www.CaregivingHopeAndHealth.com

Praise for *Caregiving*

"The opposite of love is not hate . . . it is fear. Sharon Cruse has been a visionary leader for more than thirty years, teaching caregivers how to set healthy boundaries with those we assist, so we need not fear losing ourselves in the process of caring for them. She shares her clarity, her stories, and her usable tools to help us create a kinder, more caring world for all of us. This book is her latest and most needed contribution."

—**Dr. Peter Alsop, PhD, CET**, lecturer, humorist, songwriter, parent

"Sharon Wegscheider-Cruse, world-famous author and trainer, continues through her own life experiences to grow emotionally and spiritually. She finds the words to be a leader one more time, addressing a significant passage of life that we will all be facing—the need for caregiving or to be that caregiver, and often both. As always, she takes the journey with the reader."

—**Claudia Black, PhD**, author, addiction and family trauma specialist, Senior Fellow at The Meadows addiction and psychiatric treatment program

"Sharon has always been a pioneer, forging new trails that change the destiny of generations of innumerable souls. This book represents the next chapter of that journey. Her first big gift to our world reflected on toxic caretaking and this one is on nurturing appropriate caregiving, completing the continuum. Patrick is a warm, gentle soul who is inspiring an entire new generation of caregivers to bring consciousness and wisdom in a special kind of love and caring—adding the power of technology to their caregiving toolbox for others."

—**Ted Klontz, PhD**, Associate Professor of Practice of Financial Psychology and Behavioral Finance and founder and Director, Financial Psychology Institute, Creighton University, Heider College of Business

"Sharon Wegscheider-Cruse has mentored families and professionals for decades in the art of self-care, choice-making, and negotiating intimate, professional, and extended family relationships. She now guides us along the intensely vulnerable experience of giving and receiving care as we walk into the light and darkness of physical and mental extremity. Sharon has led by her lifelong example of giving and receiving loving care. Giving voice to our often silent inner pain, Sharon again gently lights the way to respectfully walking through the last steps of our journey with those we love."

—**Carol D. Sexton, MD**, American Board of Psychiatry and Neurology

"Sharon has been both a giver and receiver of significant care over the years. In each chapter of her new book, she has stories as well as skills and perspectives that might assist all of us become better givers and receivers of caring."

—**Robert Moran, PhD**, Professor Emeritus, author of many books including *Managing Cultural Differences*

"Sharon Cruse has been given a wonderful gift. It is her ability to analyze complex feelings and behaviors and then communicate ways to live a more healthy and productive life in an easier, more understandable way. As each generation lives longer, it is crucial that we have the specific tools we need to handle the many challenging days that may come our way as we care for family and friends. We need to balance caring for others and taking care of ourselves at the same time. The caregiver must stay as healthy and strong as possible.

"Patrick Egan has been and is a loving caregiver to his parents, making it possible for them to 'age in place.' His vision with technology and useful tools for seniors makes his contribution significant. He is able to take the abstract and simplify it to manageable and usable information, especially for seniors."

—**Sandy Coletta, MA**, teacher

"Sharon is a lifelong giver and learner wrapped in wisdom and love. Her skillful writing is passionate—filled with real-life, compelling, and instructive stories.

"She and her gifted son, Pat, speak as a unique team of professionals from years of multidimensional caregiving experiences—now ready to share their gifts of cutting-edge strategies with fresh perspectives for the demands of everyday caregiving."

—**Jack Williamson**, U.S. Air Force Chaplain, Colonel (retired), former Executive Director for the National Conference on Ministry to the Armed Forces and Veterans Affairs Chaplaincy, Director of InterGen Impact—a University of Colorado Intergenerational Writing Course

"Who better than Sharon Wegscheider-Cruse and her son, Patrick Egan, to combine the practical and personal stories that bring wisdom and relief to those of us who experience the universal role of caregiver. We are not alone."

—**Marjorie Zugich**, caregiver and former
CEO of Onsite Workshops

"Sharon has advocated throughout her professional life for the health and healing of family systems. Her new book focusing on caregiving is a natural segue to continue her life's vocation."

—**Cheryl Keller,**
retired registered nurse and counselor

"Sharon has been our leader in caring for drug-addicted people and their co-dependents, and now she points the direction for our own hope and health as caregivers. This approach would be valuable for all health-care providers."

—**James W. Keller, MD**, President and CEO
Retired SEORMC, past director of Halterman
Center for Addiction Treatment

"Sharon and Pat have a unique knowledge base because Sharon has been both a caregiver and a caree, and Pat is a professional and personal caregiver. The skillful presentation provides insight and compassion for the most difficult role of all in many of our lives: that of caregiver. As a professional charged with caregiving, it is essential to take care of oneself through the process. This book offers a roadmap for caregivers—professional and personal—who are called upon to serve in ways they could never have imagined."

—**Mel Pohl, MD**, Chief Medical Officer,
Las Vegas Recovery Center, author consultant

"Sharon is a firsthand expert on caregiving and, because of her life's journey and a relatively recent traumatic accident, she has become an expert on care receiving. This newest addition to her many books, written to help all live better, more fulfilling lives, is her latest gift to humanity. As my years are increasing and my experience of caregiving is both behind me and in front of me, I am excited to learn many lessons and glean additional tools from this timely personal reflection."

—**Dee Doochin, MLAS, PCC**, life coach, daughter, wife,
mother, grandmother, great-grandmother, widow with
continued appreciation and enjoyment of life!

Caregiving

HOPE AND HEALTH
FOR CAREGIVING FAMILIES

Do you or someone you know need help?

SHARON WEGSCHEIDER-CRUSE
WITH PATRICK EGAN

Health Communications, Inc.
Deerfield Beach, Florida

www.hcibooks.com

Library of Congress Cataloging-in-Publication Data
is available through the Library of Congress

ISBN-13: 978-07573-2193-1 (Paperback)
ISBN-10: 07573-2193-3 (Paperback)
ISBN-13: 978-07573-2194-8 (ePub)
ISBN-10: 07573-2194-1 (ePub)

Publisher: Health Communications, Inc.
　　　　　3201 S.W. 15th Street
　　　　　Deerfield Beach, FL 33442–8190

Cover design by Larissa Hise Henoch
Interior design and formatting by Lawna Patterson Oldfield

This book was born of my experience.
The contents contained herein are my opinion and
not a position. It is not meant in any way to be a resource
of any scholarly presentation or medical advice.
My hope is that while reading this book, you will feel
my hand holding yours as we navigate the hard times
and share the joys of life. Where I am able,
I credit quotes and resources.

I dedicate this book
to all those who have been,
are now, or ever will be
a caregiver…

Contents

Foreword

THE RIGHT TIME
FOR THE RIGHT SOLUTIONS

When I think of a book about the impact of a caregiving experience on a family system, I can't think of better experts to write it than Sharon Wegscheider-Cruse and Patrick Egan.

A caregiving experience impacts a family system. Unfortunately, organizations—like health care, community, and faith-based—often don't have a way to help those family systems manage the experience.

Statistics show that, wow, do we need help. According to *Care Giving.com*'s 2017 Annual Family Caregiver Survey, 60 percent of respondents say they don't adequately care for themselves during caregiving and 49 percent of respondents indicate they don't receive help from other family members. Respondents offered the following explanations as to why their family members don't help:

- "They simply don't want the responsibility. They would prefer that he be in a nursing home."
- "They are busy with their own lives."
- "I'm the daughter. They *expect* this from me."
- "They live in denial."
- "They live out of town but have not even visited and don't seem interested in 'being there' for us."

Forty percent of respondents said they don't have other family members involved in discussions about care. Fifty-seven percent of respondents indicated that they don't have a back-up. Forty-five percent of respondents describe communication with other family members as "very stressful" or "stressful."

We advocate so successfully for our carees during caregiving. We speak up and out about ineffective care plans, unqualified help, illogical red tape. Ironically, we can be at a loss for words for our own needs. We can feel guilty for speaking up for ourselves because our needs seem so minimal compared to our carees'. A family caregiver recently shared that she had to cancel an outing to a friend's birthday party because of her caree's immediate and pressing need. I suggested that she share this with her family so they understand that she needs more help.

"You don't think that sounds shallow," she asked. "It seems kinda silly to be upset about missing a party."

"You're missing crucial relationships that connect you to your life," I explained. "That's important and critical information to share."

During caregiving, we are responsible for another's life. It's on us and up to us. Handing the responsibilities off to another can feel like too great a risk to take. What if something awful happens while we're at that friend's birthday party? The right language can help us understand that, as much as we want to, we can't prevent the natural cycle of life.

We also can be so tired that trying to plan and organize a break feels completely undoable. With the right words, we may find that delegating feels better and letting go seems okay. What if we could change how a family communicates? If we can change communication, would we increase the amount of help the primary family caregiver receives? When the primary family caregivers get more help, do they then have more time for their own self-care?

I believe caregiving stress is an overlooked epidemic in our communities. According to our ongoing caregiving stress survey, family caregivers rate their stress at 4.15 on a scale of 1 to 5. The source of their stress? They miss their lives. They miss downtime, free time, their own time. Chronic stress takes its toll on their health and their well-being, leaving them feeling hopeless.

We need strategies to communicate effectively and honestly about how a caregiving experience affects us—our health, our time, our well-being. Being a caregiver highlights the finite nature of time. We come to understand that we can't waste it because we never know how much is left. Sharon and Pat's book comes at the right moment, offering us encouragement, positive messages, and tools that enable us to receive help, thus giving us more time and the ability to truly enjoy it. I'm grateful to Sharon and Pat for showing us the way.

—**Denise M. Brown**,
owner of The National Caregiving Conference,
CareGiving.com, and family caregiver to her parents

FROM PAIN TO PURPOSE

How things quickly unfolded. Mom, eighty-seven years young, had taken a nasty fall and was recuperating in a residential care facility. She was not making progress and desperately wanted to be home. I had no idea how drastically things had changed with my parents' health and well-being. Living over 500 miles away, I relied on our weekly phone calls to get a sense of things. My visit painfully jolted me with a new and sad reality and now it was time to take action. Three days later, Mom was in home hospice. A week after that, Dad was in home hospice as well.

My brother, sister, and I became three of the over 40 million Americans doing caregiving. With virtually no preparation, we came together to care for our parents in the final months of their lives. We would have it no other way. My incredible sister moved into their home and became their primary caregiver. My brother, as he was available, helped with a myriad of tasks. I commuted back home every other week to provide care and support for my parents and respite for my loving sister. It was often heart-wrenching, difficult, emotionally exhausting, and overwhelming yet deeply rich and rewarding. I feel such gratitude for this opportunity.

OVERCOMING ADVERSITY

Alcoholism has hurt my family for multiple generations. I grew up with the chaos, confusion, and unpredictability of this insidious family disease. It wreaked havoc and deeply affected each one of us. Then a miracle happened. Mom and I got help and initiated a healing process for ourselves. About a year later, Dad got sober and we became a recovering family. We developed a deeper, more meaningful bond, which was a huge gift. We could talk openly about things that truly mattered in our lives. I had the parents I had always dreamed about.

I have such respect and gratitude for my parents. Their courage, strength, and tenacity were instrumental in putting our family on a new and exciting trajectory that has had a lasting, positive impact even upon my children. It was an honor to care for them. Dad wanted to stay at home and have his family be his primary caregivers. Mom wanted the same, as she had always been afraid that she would die alone. It was such a blessing to be part of a team that made their wishes come true.

OPPORTUNITY IN THE CRISIS

Once I got my bearings, I viewed this caregiving experience as a rich opportunity. Just having the time with my parents was a huge gift. We laughed, cried, and enjoyed one another's company. We reminisced about special memories and they slowly revealed more of themselves in small, subtle ways. My parents understood the reality of the situation and shared bits and pieces of their painful childhoods. We grew even closer and I came to understand and appreciate their journeys in a much deeper way.

My brother got married when I was seven years old and my sister did the same when I was eleven. In many ways, I did not get enough time with them as a kid. Our caregiving experience changed all that. While they have always had a special place in my heart, this was a chance to connect and bond in such a profound, meaningful way. We had a clear, shared purpose with the often sad and painful task and supported each other during those times of grief and emotional exhaustion. We had long talks about growing up, which helped me understand more about our family. They filled in the blanks with information I had never known, and I came to love and appreciate them even more. Because of our caregiving experience, we are much more spiritually connected.

SELF-CARE

It did not take long to realize that caregiving can be demanding, overwhelming, and exhausting. I always strived to be the best I could be for my parents, siblings, and myself. A regimen of daily self-care was a vital necessity. Eating healthy, getting plenty of rest, prayer, journaling, and reaching out for support and guidance were all key ingredients. It was also helpful to have a little time to get away—a short walk, running an errand, and reaching out to safe people. Sharon Wegscheider-Cruse, my mentor and spiritual guide, gave me valuable insight, encouragement, and helpful suggestions during our phone calls, which made such a difference for me.

Caregiving can be such a rich yet bittersweet journey. I sure wish I'd had a copy of Caregiving: Hope and Health for Caregiving Families to guide me. It is a definitive resource and road map to show you the way.

—Jerry Moe,
National Director of Children's Programs,
Hazelden Betty Ford Foundation

Acknowledgments

A book as intense and varied as this one takes the work and inspiration of many people. Caregiving was blessed with those people. First of all, it would not have come together without the skill and commitment of my personal writer and editor, Patrick Cotter. For many hours, he listened to my ideas and approaches and then helped me weave them into clear thoughts and statements. Thank you Patrick. For days and months, my coauthor, Pat Egan, and I took on massive and countless concepts on the subject of caregiving that appeared to be compelling and at sometimes overwhelming. We felt drawn to the subject personally and professionally. Those discussions developed into research and study from many diverse approaches and eventually gave birth to this book. Thank you Pat Egan.

Our ideas were passed on to Peter Vegso, who is a visionary from way back. He knows when to say yes and when to say no. He could see and feel the promise of this book coming into form, and his inspiration pulls the best out of any author. He has been a cornerstone of my career; one of the rewards of being a Health Communications author. Thank you Peter.

Then the work began. For me, it was dozens of reams of paper from Amazon, countless ink cartridges, early mornings, late nights, and a permanent perch at my second-floor computer, taking in all the weather of beautiful Colorado out my window. For Patrick and Pat, life became full of questions, more writing and rewriting. It was like the book became a member of all of our families. The book created a life of its own and we all communicated about it on what seemed like a daily basis. Eventually, the manuscript and the promise of a book was complete. Thank you to everyone involved in this process. It truly was a group effort.

I was especially happy that this was a family affair with Pat Egan, Sandy Egan, and Deb Bydlon all helping me bring a family slant to this book.

Once Christine Belleris added her magic to the process, everything really moved. She has been interested, prompt, tireless, and oh, so talented. Thank you Christine. She brought in the creative wizardry of Larissa Henoch, who wove a visual aspect into the book. Her work is so artistic and original. Thank you Larissa. Your work gives a visual punch to the concepts that are explained. And now, as I go forward with the masterful Kim Weiss, we are ready to move on with this book. Thank you Kim.

Lastly, the pure inspiration for this book comes from my

soulmate Joe Cruse, who has been both a caregiver and caree in his life, personally and professionally. With his patience, support, and love for me, I have been able to become the best person and the best writer I could ever be. We have taken our relationship, our dreams, our victories, and our struggles and turned all into adventures together, living them "one day at a time." Thank you Joe.

Introduction

There are only four kinds of people in the world: those who have been caregivers, those who are caregivers, those who will be caregivers and those who will need caregivers.

—Rosalynn Carter

After writing nineteen books, some of which became best-sellers, it seemed as though all my relevant words had been written. Yet, experience—raw, gritty, and full of gratitude—cried out from within me and would not let me rest and refrain from writing this book.

Oftentimes throughout my lifetime, life changed in a moment, but nothing stopped me completely in my tracks until a life-threatening accident about two years ago. Then came the diagnosis of the need for immediate and difficult care. I needed many kinds of help, and there was no time to plan. My family and I learned "We are all one event from a lifestyle change."

Perhaps a life-changing event has happened to you or someone you love. If so, you know many parts of the story. If not, we are in the same boat—none of us knows what the future holds. Individual dynamics come into play in a crisis, and a crisis most often affects the whole family system. A minimum of ten people are involved when a crisis strikes one person.

When a family has an emergency or even a slow-growing crisis, many people are affected: parents, daughters, sons, siblings, relatives, in-laws, and friends. For some, there may be no blood relatives, only friends. When there are no family or friends, then caregivers must rely on spiritual resources or professional care of some kind. Most often family members are the most affected when a crisis occurs.

> "One person caring about another represents life's greatest value."
> —Jim Rohn

WE ARE BORN TO CARE

Do you care? Of course, you do! You care for one person or for many people. It might be a child, parent, aunt, sibling, grandparent, grandchild, or friend. It may be that one of your greatest caring experiences is caring for one or more pets.

As humans, we have the capacity to care. Reaching out to support someone outside ourselves is caring and part of the human instinct. We relate to one another. We show we care in simple ways: through teaching, being role models, lending a helping hand, giving time, listening, and meeting specific daily needs. We show we care through offering companionship, as well as providing nourishment, transportation, and more complex aid. We help with financial care, arranging for a home or shelter, managing another's financial responsibilities, and supplying medical aid. Our caring involves support, sometimes face-to-face and other times hands-on. Sometimes caring involves distance and technology.

At some point, as the quote by Rosalynn Carter says, we are all going to be involved in either caregiving, receiving care, or both.

FROM CAREFREE TO CARE-FULL

"Make the most of your 'carefree' young life as you can."
—Anne Frank

Once upon a time, we had a "care" free life. The whole world was out there and we could play, make plans, and not worry about a thing. We could take in the happiness and excitement of the moment: ride bikes, climb trees, make mud pies, and play with friends. Many of us watched the schoolroom clock, and when 3:00 came, we ran out of the classroom and played until dinnertime. We loved peanut-butter-and-jelly sandwiches and macaroni and cheese. We rather assumed these days would go on forever.

When we earned our driver's licenses, the world opened up even more with more friends and adventures. The world was full of choices, and we didn't think much about the future. We lived day-to-day. It was a more "care" free time.

Then came a time for making choices about college, training, and relationships—finding partners to take the journey with us. So much adventure. Some chose military service, travel, and geographic changes. Others decided upon higher education with a career in mind. While still others stepped out into a variety of opportunities. It seemed the world was full of choice and adventure. Though life was changing, it was still a "care" free world.

Then, for some, in the midst of the bubble of choices, plans, and adventures, came the first major loss. We learned that not everything stays the same. "Care" free, as we knew it, changed, and a deeper part of ourselves was released.

> "Tears shed for another person (or people) are not a sign of weakness.
> They are a sign of heart."
> —José N. Harris

The first loss might have been the death of a loved one. Often, the first major loss of this kind is that of a grandparent, sibling, or other significant person. It may be loss of a limb, a sense (sight, hearing, taste, or smell). It might be an injury or illness (loss of health) or aging (loss of youth). The first experience of loss a child might experience is the death of a beloved pet.

As children, we didn't think much about our own losses. This famous quote from *Winnie the Pooh* by A. A. Milne sums up what many people discover when they experience a loss that results in caring for someone else: "Promise me you'll always remember: you're braver than you believe, and stronger than you seem, and smarter than you think." We undergo a range of emotions when our lives become full of care.

It's no accident that many adults recall this message when they experience a major life change. The wisdom of this quote has stood the test of time to support us when we find in ourselves a sadness and grief we did not know about before the loss that ended our carefree lives. That loss also brings a certain fear: fear of future loss. Loss comes in many different ways, even slowly over time.

My life-threatening accident two years ago not only changed my life in an instant, it also launched my journey of awareness about the crisis we are now experiencing in caregiving. As I experienced being a person receiving care, I saw many of the same issues in caregiving that I had seen as a young professional caregiver in the 1980s while studying and dealing with the effects on children of growing up in a family system affected by alcohol. Those effects were a form of a slow crisis steeped in loss and fear.

In both cases, millions of families nationwide experience severe stress and a lack of services to meet their needs. Both laypeople and professionals attempt to deal with a crisis for which underfunding is the norm—and systemic reform is needed. And everyone lacks a common language to talk about the situation.

Back in the 1980s, a cohesive group of people began to share their experiences, feelings, and efforts to bring help to a population troubled by the experience of growing up with alcoholism. It was a healing time. Many talented people developed and coordinated ideas, approaches, and programs through individual and collective efforts in creating literature and staging conferences. In just a few years, their efforts led to the formation of the National Association of Adult Children of Alcoholics (ACOA), of which I was one of fourteen founding board members.

Today, ACOA is recognized around the world. It simplified a complex maze of symptoms, problems, and efforts from a disconnected and wounded group of people and agencies and organizations and gave them a framework to better understand their professional and, just as importantly, their private lives. It was the birth of a new era in understanding and action in responding to alcoholism born from the experience of crisis.

BIRTH OF A NEW ERA IN CAREGIVING

My experience leads me to believe that we are on the cusp of a
new era in caregiving.

The caregiving field is in its infancy and needs to come together
in a cohesive way. We need to bring together people who are
involved with the tools that provide definition, guidance, and structure to those who need it most. We need a common language and
a simple comprehensive path, one that makes room for offshoot
trails for exploring new ground in complementary areas. This book
attempts to provide the basic path for caregiving.

A crisis exists. First, communication and structure is lacking
between caregiving agencies, conferences, podcasts, and websites. Many people, both those in caregiving situations and those

needing care, are hungry for information. Some circumstances require professional care, but these people too often go without help. The professionals are out there. The connections are lacking.

Some people navigate the caregiving maze well; others learn by trial and error; and still others have no idea where to begin. This book attempts to offer in clear language the complicated issue in our culture today. May we find the conversations and connections that will bring together as many professionals as possible.

The caregiving world is a puzzle. It is critically important, massive, disconnected, and full of amazing, well-intentioned, and hardworking people. The increasing number of people needing care is one of the fastest growing segments of our population. No accurate figure is available on the total number of formal care-givers, but one estimate states that there are 44 million unpaid caregivers. My hope is that this book starts conversations about how to come together and combine forces in the caregiving field. It's a daunting prospect, but I take heart from the words of Michael Morpugno:

> Wherever my story takes me, however dark and difficult the theme, there is always hope and redemption, not because readers like happy endings, but because I am an optimist at heart. I know the sun will rise in the morning. And there is light at the end of every tunnel.

Let's walk the tunnel together.

—*Sharon Wegscheider-Cruse*

THE CAREGIVING PUZZLE

Life changes fast.
Life changes in the instant.
You sit down to dinner and life
as you know it ends.

—Joan Didion

W e are all one event from a lifestyle change.
Have you or someone you know been through a major loss?

- accident.
- diagnosis of serious or terminal illness.
- financial loss.
- disability.
- complications of aging.

- loss of major sense—sight, hearing, sound, touch, or taste.
- sudden loss of relationship from death, divorce, or abandonment.
- diagnosis of chronic and progressive illness such as Alzheimer's or Parkinson's diseases, dementia, or MS.

My experience includes all of these losses. They happened either to me or to someone I love. My experience is my teacher and my passion for this book. Anyone who suffers through any one of these events also impacts the life of at least ten people around them. Whether family members or professional and/or volunteer caregivers, these are the people who provide care in many forms. They deliver medical care, and feed, comfort, and transport, as well as often provide financial and logistical support.

This demonstrates how fast the need for caregiving is mushrooming.

Caregiving needs can enter our lives in a moment of crisis, or they can slip in insidiously with someone needing first one thing and then another and then another. Caregivers are created instantly or developed slowly.

Either way, it's complicated. Crises and accidents catch us by surprise, which upsets routines and brings added demands on our time and energy. Slower-growing crises, such as a person experiencing undiagnosed medical issues or moving into dementia, can bring angry, confused behavior. The lack of affordable caregiving services or actual caregivers brings another layer of complication.

Adding to the complication is the fact that many professional caregivers were in caregiving positions in their families during their growing-up years. Caregiving feels natural and normal for them. Once they grow up to choose a profession, often in the care-giving field, they have great difficulty separating their professional lives from their personal lives and are prone to overwork and burn-out. This is the system we find ourselves living and working in right now. It's a staggering and powerful awareness that caregivers are also in great need of care.

This book is not about fixing anything, but it is full of tools to aid caregivers. It's more about understanding the players and the puzzle. I share my experiences with navigating both needing to be cared for at different times of my life and taking care of people at other times. You are probably in that same lifeboat with me. As the old saying goes "Don't forget to sing in the lifeboats."

CAREGIVING IS BIG BUSINESS

According to a 2015 report from the National Alliance for Caregiving and the American Association of Retired People (AARP), approximately 43.5 million caregivers in the United States provided unpaid care to an adult or child in 2014. How many more have been added since that time? It's staggering to think about the growth in caregiving. In a wider sense, businesses that care about people and the value they add are discovering that caring itself is a powerful business advantage.

I have found no comprehensive, reliable statistics about the vast numbers of professionals who work to enhance or restore the physical, psychological, intellectual, emotional, or spiritual well-being of others. They work in a wide range of fields: medicine, nursing, psychotherapy, psychological counseling, social work, and ministry. I am certain the numbers are staggering.

According to AARP, statistics tell us that 75 million baby boomers are on the verge of retirement. For the next twenty years, an average of 10,000 boomers per day will reach age sixty-five, which has historically been the threshold age of the retirement phase of life. Those born after 1960 will need to reach age sixty-seven before they receive full retirement benefits.

HOW DOES THE NEED FOR CAREGIVING ARISE?

It could be you. It could be me. It could be anyone we love. In that instant of awareness following an incident or diagnosis, caregiving is born. Once born, it tends to flourish. Two kinds of events initiate caregiving—the immediate or the unexpected. The unexpected is a realization that a loved one is truly changing: slowing, gradually, but steadily, the loved one could be slipping into dementia. Or he or she could be experiencing a permanent physical decline after a medical event—no longer able to navigate stairs, bathe without help, or manage household chores.

Both events involve a crisis of change of thought, feeling, and lifestyle. *Webster's Dictionary* describes *crisis* as "an extremely dangerous or difficult situation" in which decisions must be made.

CRISIS AND IMMEDIATE CAREGIVING

"Caregiving often starts the final walk you
have with someone you love."
—Unknown

Every crisis that gives birth to caregiving is a personal crisis. The names and details may change, but the fundamentals are similar. I like sharing stories of change from real-life examples because they bring home the impact on the upheaval in individual lives. I have changed only the names of the people involved.

DAN

Life for Dan changed in April 2017. Dan was fifty-two years old, married, with two children, and in excellent health. His dad was thrilled to be a grandpa and his mom was active and busy in her retirement life. Then came "the call." His dad had fallen in the garage and broken his hip. Dan went to his dad immediately, even though he lived fifty miles across town. He spent the initial hours in the hospital doing what he could do to ensure his dad's comfort and safety. Within four days, Dan had to make life-changing plans for the whole family. When was his dad going to be discharged? Who could take care of him when he came home? Who would take care of his mother? And what did short-term and long-term plans look like?

It was a time of chaos, confusion, and self-doubt. Dan's life went on hold, which was a problem and hardship for all. His wife had a well-paying job, and they needed her to work to contribute to the well-being of both families. Dan left his home to live with his parents for the first two weeks until his father was settled into a rehab that could see to his needs. Rehab would last only about four weeks.

Dan's elderly mother was fragile. He began the arduous task of hiring home care for her. She was well intended but not capable of taking care of herself and his father. Dan moved his mother into his home.

Dan stopped his own self-care, almost on a dime. He began to stress eat and, therefore, put on several pounds. With the weight, he lost interest in exercising and didn't take time to work out. Totally preoccupied with stress and caregiving, Dan soon developed sleeping problems. Crisis management and postponement of his own needs became the "new normal." Dan had become an immediate caregiver.

JANET

Janet also had a sudden shock when a heart problem occurred for her mother. Janet had two important and time-consuming jobs. At fifty-one, she was working as a bank manager and a YMCA evening receptionist. She was also raising two children, aged fourteen and sixteen. With one call, she learned her mother had been hospitalized and needed an emergency bypass surgery.

Janet told me she went from having a full life and schedule to needing to quit her job and be with her father and mother, who was also suffering from arthritis and limited movement. For a while, she managed to be with her parents ten hours a day and go home in the evening. Ultimately, she and her family moved into the parents' family home. They are trying to make it work. It's been difficult. The family needs are great and no one is really happy. She has let her own health slip, gaining an unhealthy amount of weight, and is often in conflict with her children, who did not want to uproot their lives.

Janet is among the millions who provide unpaid help to an ill or elderly loved one, doing everything from driving, to meal preparation, administering their medications, and helping them with whatever needs to be done.

JANICE, TOM, AND LISA

Janice, sixty, and Tom, seventy, are a bubble couple and have been for about twenty years. A bubble couple is one in which the relationship comes first for each partner; they create their own protective bubble where each feels safe and secure. They thought it would all be great forever. They are living in a warm climate and built the perfect house in a fifty-five-plus community. They enjoy their neighbors. Janice volunteers at the local library and works for causes she believes are important. She and Tom used to regularly play cards, but they are starting to get confused, and the card games aren't going well at the moment.

Janice is happy with her neighbors but is estranged from her son, Danny. This causes her a great deal of sorrow and anger. Her daughter, Lisa, thirty-eight, has been trying to help her mother's sorrow and worries about her dad, Tom. Since being concerned about her parents, Lisa has spent less time at the gym; she feels her outlet has been "dinners out," and she is concerned about the extra weight she is carrying. Lisa is slowly becoming the caregiver.

MELISSA

Melissa, thirty-one, is a baby boomer and moved to a different state from her parents when her husband, Lee, was promoted. She knows her parents are getting older, and she feels guilty that they are so lonely for her, their only daughter. Melissa also has two little girls of her own, her parents' only grandchildren. She feels that she is being pulled apart by the needs of her parents, her husband, and her girls.

She orders and pays for Meals on Wheels for her parents, sends an e-mail or calls her mom every day, and talks to her dad a couple of times a week. She sends ideas of things they can do and tries to support them from a distance. She visits and takes the girls to see them as often as she can. Melissa and Lee rarely talk about getting away "just for them." Lee is starting to feel abandoned and lonely, and Melissa thinks she is dancing as fast as she can. Melissa has become a caregiver.

SHIRLEY AND MIKE

Shirley, sixty-two, and Mike, seventy-one, have a familiar story. They raised three children and welcomed seven grandchildren. Early retirement was the beginning of the bubble, and they loved

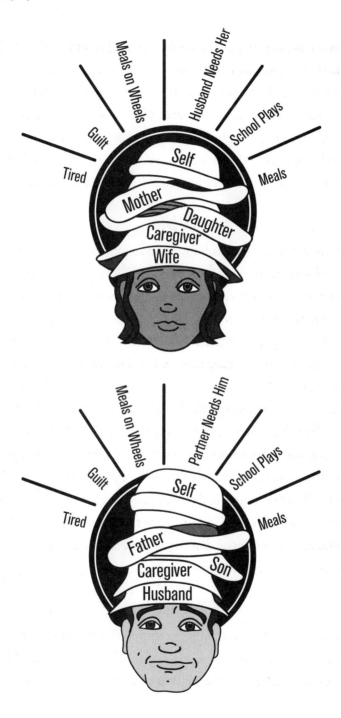

it. The grandchildren were young and fun, and Shirley and Mike were young enough to enjoy those early years. It was a magical time. They moved and downsized as they got older and the grandchildren started to grow up.

Then one day Shirley was diagnosed with breast cancer. That changed the bubble from leisure and grandparenting to doctor appointments, Mike's fears, and increasing distance from their son, David, thirty-five, who had become busier in his job and looking after the needs of his children. Within a short period, Shirley became frightened and worried most of the time. Tied up in the needs of her care, Mike was angry and starting to get confused. Their family grew more distant—simply because each was just trying to meet their own needs.

Soon after Shirley's breast cancer diagnosis, Mike suffered a heart attack. And in the blink of the eye, he was gone. Shirley felt terrified. Could she take care of herself? How could she see her grandchildren? What was to become of her? She missed Mike, who had always been there for her. David tried to help but felt pulled in many directions. David was on the brink of becoming a caregiver.

ANNA

Anna, forty-three, was the firstborn child and always the apple of her parents' eye. Anna was almost like a third person in her parents' marriage. She and her mom loved to do things together, and they had always been close. They always shared thoughts and feelings. Four years separated Anna and her next sibling. Anna's two younger brothers were closer to dad, who loved sports, fishing, and the outdoors. They all live within a thirty-mile radius.

When dad's behavior started changing, Anna and her mom shared their concerns with each other. To protect the privacy of their dad, a respected businessman, they didn't share much with the rest of the family. Anna and her mom worried about the changes in Dad, such as forgetting details of events, not paying some bills, and getting lost on the computer. They began to cover for him. This went on a few months before they realized that his driving was erratic. The first confrontation came when they asked him to give up his car keys. After some grunting and groaning, he handed them over.

Anna's mom then realized that her life was changing even more. She was the sole driver in the family. Anna's mom wasn't getting any younger, and suddenly both Anna and her mother had become caregivers. Anna realized that she was a double caregiver, for both her mom and dad—just at different levels. Anna finally reached out to her brothers and asked for help. They did not respond with any help even though they lived close by. They offered her advice and support, but they did not step forward. She was left with the day-to-day support and felt abandoned, bewildered, and alone. That situation continues today. Anna's dad has drifted into a "world of his own," and though her mom is trying hard, she often feels overwhelmed. There aren't clear answers for anyone in this family. Anna is a double caregiver.

BARRY AND CARL

Barry, fifty-six, and Carl, sixty-eight, have been together as a loving couple for thirty-three years. They do not have children. In the early days, they were both employed, had many friends, and entertained often. It was a fun, social life. Then Carl was diagnosed with a progressive disease. Barry was right there for him and remains so.

As Carl's illness has progressed, they entertain less and have lost many of their friends. Barry is still connected to some friends but knows great loneliness. He still wants and needs to travel, which he does some through his work. Carl can do increasingly less for himself, so their life is becoming more isolated. They love and are present for each other, but it's a hard life. Barry has become a caregiver and has shaped his life around Carl.

JOHN AND LUCY

Last is wealthy John, seventy-two, and Lucy, seventy-one. They are each other's caregivers. They both have physical problems. They both have brilliant minds but are slipping into dementia at the same time. On good days, they have managed to hire outside help to come in and assess their situation. They hire professional help for driving, financial management, and decision making. They have a housecleaner and other help they need to function from day-to-day. They have two sons.

While the couple can function, their emotional needs and social needs go unmet. The two sons keep their distance but check in on them often enough to ensure they are safe and getting the help they need. Both boys are in a position to inherit the funds this couple will leave behind and are reluctant to help them get into a care situation that might better meet their needs but also costs more money. It is a lonely situation. This is caregiving with the least engagement.

"The worst thing in the world is watching someone you love
suffer in pain when there is nothing you can do to stop it."
—*Vanessa Wilhoit*

OF CAREGIVING AND CARE RECEIVING

"When written in Chinese, the word *crisis* is
composed of two characters—one represents danger
and the other represents opportunity."
—*John Kennedy*

As we enter the world of caregiving, it's easy to see how families, couples, and groups become overwhelmed when they realize the range of needs. As this awareness and information are shared between the one receiving care and those giving care, the whole process can become confusing and complicated. Misunderstandings and chaos often surface, and the whole process becomes messy. This book is about navigating the messiness and bringing order to this complex subject and growing problem in our culture.

I spent many years at the feet of mentor and family therapist Virginia Satir, who taught me a set of principles that has taken me to where I am today. As my experience has proven to me, she was spot-on in her values and thoughts. In a workshop in Berkley, California, where we were sharing the stage, she said, "There are stages in life that can provoke a crisis as an experience of opportunity. A crisis is a disruption of life as we know it, and each crisis looks and feels different, although patterns can develop."

In whatever circumstances we find ourselves, the opportunity presents itself in how we reframe the crisis into something manageable. Following are a few crises and opportunities that are common in the course of many lives.

1. Time of conception by our parents—and what was going on in their lives at the time of our conception.
2. Our moms' pregnancies and our births—the earliest influence on us, followed by learning the skills for eating, walking, speaking, and eliminating.
3. An official connection outside the family—day care, nursery school, teachers, and friends.
4. Adolescence—and all it brings or causes.
5. Adulthood and moving away from home, which is the beginning of independence. This is often one of the first of ongoing grief experiences, which can build within us resiliency, according to many studies.
6. Marriage or partnering will bring another system and people into the mix. Choosing to stay single will also develop some kind of system. Very few people tend to choose absolute isolation, with no human involvement. Connections may tighten within the family of origin, or new systems are developed.
7. Becoming a parent causes the immediate inclusion of grandparents. Grandparenting is full of privilege, as well as traps, and love beyond belief.
8. Then comes caregiving of some kind, paid and unpaid.
9. Followed by the aging process for every single person. Change and differentness are probably most exposed in this time of the family, couple, and process. Some become the wise elders, some grow distant, and some

become capable of draining the life out of the system they are part of.

10. Finally comes death of a family member, and everything often shifts again. The primary constant is grief, loss, change, and adaptation. In between is joy, excitement, celebration, milestones, victory, and great happiness.

Every child born into this world comes into a different grouping and a different environment, even if born to the same two parents. The blueprint and the context are different for every human being. Some people say that the first child is different because they are the only children who are born into a coupling. The first child is every mother's and every father's guinea pig, resulting in handicaps and opportunities. It can be no other way. However, it presents an opportunity to parents for a unique adventure as this child develops.

IDENTIFYING THE
CAREGIVERS

*Caring can be learned by all human beings,
can be worked into the design of every life,
meeting an individual need as well as
a pervasive need in society.*

—Mary Catherine Bateson

Who are the caregivers? When the need arises, the varied collection of people who need to get involved seem to appear in a combination of paid and unpaid caregiving jobs. The paid include doctors, emergency vehicle drivers, nurses, home health aides, and others. The unpaid are typically family members and friends. Together they form a whole group. This is when we realize that no man or woman is an island.

My personal experience began when I was a caregiver in my home, responding to the many crises that my family members experienced: my mother's heart disease, my sister's depression and subsequent cancer, and my daughter's illness. My caregiving reached a crescendo when my soul mate began suffering with chronic obstructive pulmonary disease (COPD), chronic bronchitis, pain in his chest from a fall, heart failure, and depression. This eight-week episode culminated with my having a fainting episode that led to a life-threatening fall down a flight of stairs, to be followed by my soul mates' additional diagnosis of Parkinson's disease.

It was a very difficult time, and it was clear that caregiving is a commitment, hard work, and relentless, but also rewarding. It is important to remember that caregiving is also one of life's greatest experiences, a powerful opportunity for growth when faced, accepted, and worked through.

Caregiver Characteristics

Whether caregivers are professional or nonprofessional, paid or unpaid, they share the same characteristics. Caregivers:

1. respond to a need because they personally care;
2. are often over-responsible;
3. provide care even when their own needs go unmet;
4. often have happy outsides and painful insides;
5. sometimes react rather than respond;
6. feel like there isn't enough of themselves to go around;
7. have an exaggerated sense of power and control;

8. seek approval from others and do not want to disappoint;
9. feel like whatever they do isn't enough; and
10. are tired and worn out much of the time.

Caregiver Rewards

In the process of caregiving, however, are rich rewards. Caregivers:

1. often experience quality intimate relations with the family;
2. develop a broad cultural perspective;
3. become aware of what is truly essential and nonessential in life;
4. develop a kindness and compassion unknown to many;
5. know how to give back;
6. know the purpose and meaning of life;
7. have few regrets;
8. realize they do the best they can;
9. develop increasing sensitivity; and
10. develop gratitude.

FORMAL "PAID" CAREGIVERS

"No one cares how much you know, until they know how much you care."
—*Theodore Roosevelt*

Many paid caregivers are compensated through insurance/Medicare or some other care-paying system. Medicare covers most hospice care. The caregiver can also be paid privately for many other services he or she provides. Every situation is different; each person has to work out a payment profile for the variety of caregivers involved.

THE LANGUAGE OF CAREGIVING

Listening to people talk about caregiving was quite complicated for me just after I was injured in my fall. My experience in the addiction field had already taught me that language can be defining, confusing, and helpful all at the same time. Understanding the difference between words and phrases, such as *addict, chemically dependent, identified patient, family system, roles that family members take on, treatment modality, support group, therapeutic group,* and *12-step modality,* clarified situations and made conversations regarding the person/circumstance directed and understandable.

In the hospital and during rehab and ongoing treatment after my fall, I eventually became familiar with much of the language of caregiving from the professionals working with me. This was the hard way to pick up the jargon; therefore, I have included some of the common caregiving language, describing what I learned and experienced as I went through it.

DEFINING CAREGIVING AND CAREGIVER ROLES

I define caregiving as the full range of activities one provides to an individual or group of people. Formal caregiving involves paid positions that are part of an umbrella system. These include the following:

- **Emergency First Responders:** ambulance drivers, doctors, and nurses.
- **Hospital Personnel:** attendants who transport patients in wheelchairs and gurneys, bring blankets, and offer comfort.
- **Hospitalists:** doctors employed by hospitals who work with a medical team or the patient's primary doctor to determine the length of the hospital stay and what insurance will and will not cover.
- **Chaplains:** they often offer to meet your spiritual needs.
- **Social Workers/Case Managers:** they determine who is currently involved in your case and how to proceed from stage to stage. This person tries to plan a package for the patient on discharge day to move into another level of care.
- **Medical Transportation Drivers:** they transport patients from one facility to another.
- **Psychologists:** they talk to patients (and sometimes listen) about their emotions and understanding of what is happening to them.

- **Primary Doctors:** they are sometimes involved (usually in an office setting) and will communicate by fax and phone. Rarely seen in a hospital or rehab facility, they take care of the patient when released from the facility.
- **Wound-Care Specialists:** medical specialists who manage wound care. Sometimes it is a nurse, and some settings have specialists in this area.
- **Nurses:** they include a variety of registered nurses (RN) and certified nursing assistants (CNA).
- **Physical Therapists:** they are often the most present professionals involved in many rehab centers, and patients see them on a regular basis.
- **Housekeepers:** they visit patients' rooms, sometimes twice daily.

GOING HOME

When moving back home from rehab, most people need another team of paid caregivers. Here the care is very individualized, depending on the county, state, and insurance, as well as the availability of local resources and personal financial ability. Going home began an intensive and wonderful experience for me; however, this phase can easily cause some confusion. I was told I would need the following services:

- Vocational therapy for functional, psychological, cognitive, and emotional help. I needed to overcome my fear of falling up or down stairs. Even though I was unconscious before I fell, my fear was at an unconscious level. It was some time before I could go up and down stairs easily and without extra caution. Walking safely, without fear, with the aid of a walker was very important at this time.

- Occupational therapy assisted me with functioning at my optimal level while going through and following physical therapy. For me, this meant relearning how to shower and bathe while in great pain and how to prevent a second fall. Just sitting up, standing up, getting in and out of bed, and getting dressed and undressed when unable to move in a familiar way is a whole new set of skills. It also meant learning to keep a walker with me at all times and taking no risks, such as trying to walk again too soon.

- Physical therapy involves relearning physical skills and building strength, mobility, function, and eventually healing and moving with ease, free of pain. I practiced and relearned all the skills I had taken for granted until my body regained its memory of movement.

- The case worker manages all these therapies, arranging appointments and sessions, also serving as a social worker to address the patient's feelings about what is happening. My experience was absolutely wonderful. My physical, occupational, and vocational therapists came to my home for five weeks—a combination of four therapists coming three times a day during that time. Then I graduated to walking on my own, having the ability to get in and out of a car, going up and down stairs, and generally managing the basics on my own.

It would have been much easier for me had I known all of this before the accident. It was definitely "learning while experiencing." My hope is that these terms and descriptions prepare you or someone you love to better navigate the system.

"There is no education like adversity."
—*Benjamin Disraeli*

FRIENDS AS CAREGIVERS

"Time and good friends are two things that become
more valuable the older you get."
—*Anonymous*

We need our friends most in times of crisis or illness. It's worth every ounce of effort to keep those relationships alive and well nurtured. However, while providing heavy caregiving, it's hard to do everything. Too often, we neglect our friendships. It just seems too frivolous to spend time connecting with friends and sharing a dinner, a phone call, or a walk when the days already feel like they are thirty-six hours long. But that may be when we most need and cherish a friend's presence.

Really close friends who love you "wait." They time their visits and calls when they know you can receive them. They also don't go away even if you don't have much time for them "at the moment." While it's easier than ever today to travel to see friends, many people with caregiving responsibilities travel less and less. The second half of this book will offer many ways to help nurture friendships and keep them alive.

A large number of friends seems to matter less than a few important ones. Finding and then keeping friends who "calm our soul" and nurture us can be challenging for people with busy lifestyles. First, it seems like we have less contact, and with less contact, we have less to share. All too soon it seems like it isn't worth the effort to water, fertilize, weed, and manage a friendship, just like a plant. But it is necessary.

Another problem is when friendships have shallow roots, or friends are simply acquaintances we spend time with at events, or people we engage with only through hobbies or sports. We might easily lose those relationships because we don't have a deep enough connection to stay friends.

INFORMAL PAID (PRIVATE PAY) CAREGIVERS

"Never believe that a few caring people can't change the world.
For indeed, that's all who ever have."
—*Margaret Mead*

In the last few years, an entire industry has arisen that offers a multitude of caregiving services that in former times hospitals and the catchall phrase *old folks homes* would have provided.

"Sometimes people can't define what they need,
but when relief comes, they know it."
—*Anonymous*

I had little awareness of the armies of informal and private-pay agencies that have sprung up in many parts of the country and are growing as fast as our population is aging. They go by many different names and are more plentiful in more densely populated areas. Regardless of their structure, these agencies provide services to aid those in need. Most of them are a business; therefore, they expect to make a profit.

Some agencies specialize in one area while others offer a range of services. The services are usually paid by the hour. Rates depend on the level of training and certification of the individual providers. Some informal paid caregivers become regular members of a caregiving team, and others help on a "when needed" arrangement.

Informal, private-pay caregiving services include the following:

- Home health care provided by wound specialists and physical, vocational, and psychological therapists deliver services to or in the home.
- Transportation—cars, buses, and limousines—companies provide services for post-surgical and aging populations. Some require a medical diagnosis to provide their service, while others are for hire, requiring only payment.
- Case management, private-practice social work, and resource-sharing individuals listen to your specific needs and put together a team for you.
- Nursing services and care are provided in your home and are paid by the hour.
- Medical management looks after organizing and ordering prescriptions and scheduling visits. Hired by the hour, they listen to your needs and take you to your medical appointments, watch and listen to the care, feedback, and instructions your doctors and nurses give, order your

medications, and set up your pill boxes for you. Each state has different requirements for this type of home care, so users must check local regulations.

- Light housekeeping.
- Food preparation.

My personal experience has been to hire home health nursing services, medical management, light cooking/food preparation and housekeeping, and transportation. It takes the edge off "too busy" days when ten things need to be done at once. It's a great service offering, and my experiences have been mostly top-notch, despite a couple of disappointments.

THE UNPAID FAMILY CAREGIVER

"Have patience and love—remember how you will want
someone to treat you when you need care."
—*Sharon Cruse*

Perhaps nothing challenges a family more than when one of the
family members needs caregiving. Family caregivers make up the
lion's share of a massive, unpaid, invisible workforce. The latest
statistics at the time of this writing are provided in the report
Caregiving in the U.S., a 2015 study by the National Alliance for
Caregiving and the AARP. The numbers will have certainly grown
dramatically by now.

Unpaid Caregivers in the United States by the Numbers

- Approximately 43.5 million caregivers have provided unpaid care to an adult or child in the twelve months prior to being surveyed for the Caregiving in the U.S. study.
- About 34.2 million Americans have provided unpaid care to an adult age fifty or older in the twelve months prior to being surveyed.
- The majority of caregivers (82 percent) care for one other adult, while 15 percent care for two adults.
- Approximately 39.8 million caregivers provide care to adults (aged 18+) with a disability or illness.
- About 15.7 million adult family caregivers care for someone who has Alzheimer's or dementia.

CAREGIVING AS THE ULTIMATE FAMILY EXPERIENCE

"Some people care too much. I think it's called love."
—*Winnie the Pooh*

Individual stories often illustrate best how caregiving unfolds in a family. Through caregivers' stories, we can see the breadth and depth of the impact on families—the love that sustains them.

DONNA

Donna's story teaches us how easy it is for the whole family to be involved when one of their members changes. Picture a mobile with five or six butterflies hanging from it. Remove one butterfly and the whole mobile changes balance.

Donna's caregiving reflects the experience of many women. She married Ray when she was a young girl. Donna settled into the role of wife and mother as well as being a young woman with good business sense. While Ray was the primary breadwinner with a very successful career, Donna made good money in a small business she started. She juggled motherhood, work, and the family's social life. Donna hosted parties and get-togethers for two families—her family of origin and the family she created with Ray. Everyone liked being around Donna. All would say about her, "What a good cook," "What a fun time," "Such a good mom and family member," and "Isn't she just the greatest?" Life went on like this for a long time.

When Ray began to experience memory loss and private temper tantrums, Donna assumed he was just getting older and overlooked early signs of significant change. She was getting older as well, and she wasn't changing. When Ray's driving became erratic and he had a car accident, Donna spoke up and demanded he give up his keys to the car. Then the troubles began for the two of them. Ray accused Donna of controlling his life—all the way from his driving to smaller incidents in the house. Ray quit being the gentle loving man he had always been and became rigid and controlling. At first Donna covered it up because she was embarrassed. When she started telling the family how it really was, they were slow to believe the situation was as bad as she said. One daughter told Donna that she felt that Donna was unfair to her father and should be more helpful.

Soon the children were taking sides, each interpreting what was happening through their personal lenses. Family relationships experienced great strain until finally a trusted family friend offered to assist the family to get professional help and advice. Eventually,

Ray made plans to go to a memory care center. However, it was not soon enough. Donna had a heart attack and died while Ray was still in the planning stage for the memory home. The family went into two crises in quick succession.

This story is repeated all too often. We all know stories of when the caregiver has a sudden debilitating loss—or dies—before the caree. Stress and poor self-care can lead to dire outcomes.

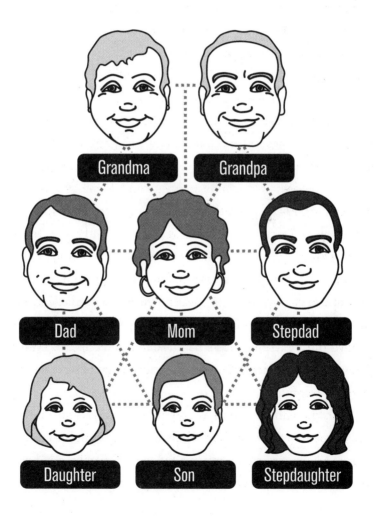

CAREGIVER ROLES IN FAMILIES AND GROUPS

"Alone we can do so little; together we can do so much."
—*Helen Keller*

No matter what the configuration of the people nearest the one who needs care, a system of care emerges for that person. Sometimes the caregivers are family members, paid caregivers, unpaid caregivers, or volunteers. In every case, a system evolves in which people step into various roles. It becomes easier to understand the system and how it operates when we understand the roles and how they interact. Naming the roles is the first step. The *caree* is the person who needs help. The *caregiver* is the person who gives care of any kind. There may be one or several caregivers. Each situation is different.

Beyond caree and caregiver, people who step up to help fall into specific roles, each one identified by a natural "pattern of behavior." Behavior patterns tend to emerge in crises. Following are four caregiver roles (patterns of behavior) that often emerge when a crisis or slow-moving illness first invades the family:

- **Team Captain:** This person takes on the role of being dependable, hands-on, and can be counted on to be organized and to get things done. Someone needs to call the shots. On the outside, the Team Captain appears to be organized and efficient. On the inside, he or she feels lonely, scared, and tired.
- **Helper:** This role supports the Team Captain and carries out assigned tasks. Those who take on this role are very important and much needed. Helpers jump in and do what needs to be done. Sometimes they are paid, and

sometimes they are volunteers. On the inside, they feel
satisfied and know they do what they can. They also sometimes feel inadequate compared with others.

- **Avoider:** Those who seem less caring take this role. They
stay away from the action and rarely get much praise or
blame. They support, or ignore, from a distance, whether
geographic or emotional. On the inside, the Avoider feels
angry, inadequate, and afraid.
- **Blamer:** Whenever things do not work out, the Blamer finds a
way to find fault with another member of the family system
for whatever doesn't work. They excuse themselves from
responsibility. On the inside they feel angry, guilty, and sad.

Caregivers take on parts of each role or stick to one that works
well for them. How they act out their roles can be blatant or subtle
and unspoken. They can change roles at different times of their
lives and in different circumstances. Finding balance becomes very
hard for caregivers, and fatigue and burnout are great risks for caregiving individuals and families. No one is, or can do, everything.
Burnout is common, and feelings are often confused.

The same blood that holds families together can tear them
apart. Family systems are alike and different in many ways. Understanding and communication are needed to draw the best from
each individual so that the system can function when one of them
needs care. We'll revisit the family as caregivers in Chapter 8 as my
soul mate and children share their experiences as family caregivers
when I was the caree. In Chapter 9, we'll see how building bridges
in families—and among other caregiver groups—can enhance the
team's performance.

TEAM CAPTAIN

BLAMER
Criticizing

AVOIDER
Back
to Career
and Family

HELPER

AGENCY ROLES

Roles that have been established in family systems over the years move into professional patterns as well. To know oneself personally is to know oneself professionally. In my own company many years ago, I used the same principles that I used in family therapy sessions and took them to agencies and corporate businesses to better understand how

- board of directors worked with one another;
- teams function in the workplace; and
- employers and employees are involved with one another.

One can see how, in the caregiving field, confusion, chaos, and lack of management emerge when personal and professional roles mix together. Bringing everything into the open, naming it, and clearly communicating are important tasks. This is true in all business but especially in caregiving.

The same system and role development occur in agencies, hospitals, and any place a group gathers to provide care. It only makes sense that all groups are simply people who came from family systems, and they often bring their family roles (patterns of behavior) with them into adulthood and into their professional lives. It is only when people pause to assess their personalities and relationships to others that they can see how they play into each system.

It only makes sense that all groups are simply people who came from family systems, and they often bring their family roles (patterns of behavior) with them into adulthood and into their professional lives.

An illness, accident, or agency crisis can push the tipping point in any direction. Family members or employees who provide care together or work together can evoke guilt, fear, envy, anger, and sadness in one another. Each connection has the power to build or destruct. That is why family and professional relationships are so tender.

Each person needs to become a choice maker for himself or herself. Then if they want to be in a relationship, they will need to consider the wants and needs of others. Problems arise when the balance between caring for oneself and caring for the other becomes totally out of balance.

Problems arise when the balance between caring for oneself and caring for the other becomes totally out of balance.

Caregiving System Dynamics Summary

1. Family members and agency employees take on roles and develop a unique system.
2. Every person in that system has her or his own thoughts and feelings and develops a unique way of responding to others.
3. To be successful in a family or an agency, each member needs to consider the wants and needs of one another.
4. Every member of the group will affect each person.
5. Each person will change and develop over time and in changing circumstances.

Makeup of Family Units Varies

1. Single Family (mom, dad, children).
2. Blended Family (mom, stepmom, dad, stepdad, children).
3. Gay Family (two moms or two dads, children).
4. Single-Parent Family (parent and child/children).
5. Adult-Only Family (no children).
6. Chosen Family (groups of people without blood connection).

No matter the configuration, people are in one another's lives —for better or for worse—for their entire lives. Even if a family member dies, death will end a life but not a relationship or memory. Perhaps

Death will end a life but not a relationship or memory.

you have done the necessary work to create a functional family unit. Then again, maybe many circumstances have kept that from happening. It is never too late to begin the work of creating a functional family unit, whatever the present circumstances are, and go forward. That work includes identifying any ways that would increase communication, understanding, and care for each other. While we cannot change the past, we can change our thinking *about* the past. We might be able to reframe some childhood pain through understanding and acceptance.

> "If you are going through hell, keep going."
> —*Winston Churchill*

> "It's never too late to have a happy childhood."
> —*Tom Robbins*

VOLUNTEERS

> "Volunteers do not necessarily have the time;
> they just have the heart."
> —*Elizabeth Andrews*

The millions of volunteers providing caregiving throughout our culture still tend to make themselves available primarily through the formal organizations that most of us are familiar with. Some of the best known include the following:

- American Red Cross
- Habitat for Humanity
- Peace Corps
- American Cancer Society
- Kiwanis
- Rotary
- Various shelters
- Homeless homes
- Domestic Violence Centers

- AARP
- Shriners
- Local food banks and kitchens

Everyone finds their niche regarding donating time and money, and everyone finds a second niche when they need the services themselves. Helping others is part of the soul's development and can last a lifetime—and change in form throughout a lifetime.

Creativity was always part of giving. I was seventeen when I joined Big Brothers and Big Sisters. I had a Little Sister for several years. Her name was Henrietta. She helped make me a better person. In my teens, my family and I took in dogs to give them homes. As a college student, I worked in homeless kitchens and helped prepare box lunches for kids. As an adult, my helping included teaching Sunday school in my church, being a member of a Kindness Group that prepared packages to send home with newborns and moms who had little to no resources, making food for temporary residents of Ronald McDonald House, and more. Later in life, I fostered children for a while, and hosted foreign exchange students (fourteen months at a time from eight countries). These volunteer positions provided great personal fulfillment.

I list these projects because I wasn't aware that these activities are ways of caregiving until I started this book. I thought of them only as lucky activities because they taught me much and connected me with amazing people. I am much more aware today as I have needed some of that volunteerism in my own life.

Some ways that caregiving has come full circle is the wonderful people in my county who drive seniors to medical appointments.

Sometimes the volunteers are younger than their carees, sometimes the same age or older. The only difference is that they are in the giving stage right now, and it means so much to someone who needs that kind of care.

Someone near to me is at a time of life when getting out and about is difficult. He is a brilliant and curious man who needs mental stimulation from others. Through an aging agency volunteer group, he has found a wonderful companion who matches his ability to wonder, think, and explore possibilities and concepts. A couple of stimulating conversations a week is like a rainbow after a summer storm. Magnificent and awe-inspiring.

> "Volunteers don't get paid, not because they are worthless,
> but because they're priceless."
> —*Sherry Anderson*

FELLOWSHIP IN GATHERINGS

LUCY

Lucy is only sixty-four. Until recently, she was walking every day and enjoying baking. She always had a treat for anyone who stopped by. From cookies to homemade bread, she would receive visitors, who liked to sample her creative goodies. Her sense of humor made going to her home a treat for everyone.

On a warm summer day, Lucy was baking bread and suddenly collapsed, unconscious. It was not until a neighbor stopped over to see her and called 911 that she got help.

Lucy had suffered a severe stroke. She isn't old enough for senior assistance, so her need for caregiving consumed her savings and her small income each month. Once she returned home, she hired caregivers, who visited regularly to take care of many of her basic needs. She also belongs to a wonderful church, where volunteers came in weekly to offer her warmth, love, and time.

Lucy has neither children nor living siblings. She was and is dependent solely on community caregivers. Her situation is quite common. What separates her story from many others is her age. She is young to need to depend on so many caregivers.

GRANDPARENTS

"Grandparents make the world a little softer, a little kinder, a little warmer."
—*Irish proverb*

TED

Ted, in his seventies, is a retired attorney. He and his wife, Sara, in her sixties, have loved the good retirement life. Their family home is in a woody suburb in the Midwest. They also own a condo in California where they live during the winter months. They love to travel and have set aside money to help educate their grandchildren. These are their golden years. That is, they were until their son and daughter-in-law were killed in a car accident. The accident shattered the entire family. Ted and Sarah flew back to the Midwest to be with their grandchildren and to support them in the loss of their parents. Two years have gone by and they are still there.

They hired day-to-day help for the two children, who were then in junior and senior high school. But they couldn't bear being so far from them so much of the time. They sold their California home and moved back to the Midwest to live with the grandchildren. They are aging and worry about the long-term effects this will have on the grandchildren as time passes. In many ways, they have become caregivers while also recognizing they will soon need care for themselves. This situation was not part of their retirement plans.

COACHES AND LEADERS

"Coaching is an action, not a title. And actions result in successes."
—Byron and Catherine Pulsifer

Coaching sports at a local high school, Mike was always available whenever a student needed something. Students counted on him for rides, skilled coaching, or a snack bar here and there. He never saw himself as a caregiver, and I don't know if he does to this day. He naturally thought of others. Mike was a good friend with an open ear and heart. He taught and coached until he retired.

Is it any wonder that after retirement, he became a volunteer driver giving other seniors rides to medical appointments and just stopping by for a visit? Giving of himself has been a way of life for Mike as long as I have known him. He is an example of a true volunteer caregiver in the purest form.

HELP! I HURT:
BEING THE CAREE IS HARD

Maybe life isn't about avoiding the bruises;
maybe it's about collecting the scars
to prove we showed up for it.

—Hannah Brencher

Researching and sharing about what it is like to be a person who needs care from another, as well as a system of caregivers, triggered a startling awareness in me. Very little information and storytelling comes directly from the caree. I can describe the outsides of some carees but very little on their thoughts, feelings, and needs. Information is available regarding their diagnosed physical illness, their supposed psychological needs for care, and their families and systems who provide the care. But little or nothing is available about the people themselves who need care.

At different levels, they have myriad feelings, thoughts, and needs. Even though they need care in some area(s) of their lives, they can be contributing, fun and funny, talented, intelligent, and interesting. Their input needs to be a part of every caregiving team.

When I became a caree, not only did I change but also my world and relationships changed around me. I became one of "them" or "they." In my room in the hospital/rehab, I could hear myself being referred to as "Room 113," rather than by my name. That was startling, especially when my nurses and aides wrote their names on the whiteboard when they were on duty.

Experiencing a life-changing event that requires a person to receive care is not easy. Needing care is a difficult place to live and is sometimes a source of shame and feelings of loss. Work, activity, and connection give a person purpose and meaning. To have that stripped away brings emotional pain; life gets emptier. This shouldn't be, for no matter what injury or illness the person has suffered, they are still people of value. They can share their creativity, fun, stories, wisdom, experience, and hope and enrich someone else's life.

People who suffer are curious, scared, angry, guilty, ashamed, excited, generous, and afraid. They have all the normal feelings everyone else has. If they are on a great deal of medication, some of their feelings might be accessed more slowly or be a bit repressed. However, it might not be much different for a number of the general population, as their feelings are inhibited because of addictions to screens (TV, computer, tablet, smartphone); use of drugs (prescription and illegal); or misuse of alcohol, work, or food. In the end, everyone needs to work at creating and maintaining connections, and carees need to be part of that effort.

PUBLIC AND PRIVATE CHANGES FOR CAREES

Some of life's changes are very public. They can include hospitalization, accident, downsizing, divorce, physical and mental challenges, addiction, loss of job, death, dementia, and obesity. When the changes are public, there is often shame, change of lifestyle, grief, and obvious consequences. It is hard to keep them secret. But the people experiencing the change still need care—and they need to share about their feelings.

When changes are private, resulting effects still exist, but they are different from the public ones. It is quite common for people to feel responsible for their illnesses. They may believe that they could have prevented them, or that they have become weaker as a result. They may want to conceal their illnesses—or their slow loss of mental or physical health—for as long as possible, to keep it and the effects secret. In Chapter 9, we talk more about building the bridges that enable connections, which ease the pain of illnesses and loss.

In both cases, part of healthy caregiving—and receiving—is acknowledging the change and talking about it.

In both cases, part of healthy caregiving—and receiving— is acknowledging the change and talking about it.

Identifying Obvious Carees

Carees range in age, need, severity of an issue, reason to need care, financial means, family involvement, awareness, and ability. A person can become a caree from a range of events, situations, and illnesses, including the following:

1. injuries following an auto or sports accident
2. chronic illness (such as multiple sclerosis, amyotrophic lateral sclerosis, advanced heart conditions, advanced diabetes, mental illness, cancers, stroke, and many more)
3. conditions connected to aging (Alzheimer's, dementia, Parkinson's disease, and many more)
4. post-surgical care
5. disabilities (physical, emotional, or psychological) in children or adults
6. needs of parents who live far away
7. need for management of financial situations
8. loss of major senses (hearing, sight, touch, sound, and taste)
9. children
10. complications with aging

It's important not to categorize everyone who identifies with one or more of the above needs. Some people have the resources and people in their lives to fill all their needs before any of the complications or needs are felt. But it's also true that many don't have either the resources or the team nearby to fulfill all their needs. In some cases independence can be recovered, but it takes time. In other cases, full independence cannot be restored. Everyone experiences a different situation. It is important that we all know, explore, and understand the thoughts and feelings of each caree.

Communication and connections between carees and caregivers are essential, and when properly understood, the caree and

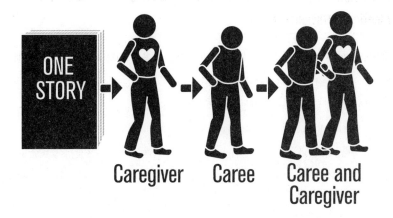

caregiver might realize that both are on a journey that shares similarities. Both the caree and the caregiver share some of the same feelings:

- **Fear:** This is new territory and a lifestyle change for both.
- **Wishfulness:** They wish things could be as they "used to be."
- **Helplessness:** They feel helpless in some ways.
- **Love:** They love the other, even when they sometimes don't feel love.
- **Distress:** Sometimes everything feels like "too much."
- **Uncertainty:** They don't know how or when to ask for help sometimes.
- **Loneliness:** They feel lonely and not heard sometimes.
- **Confusion:** They feel like "What happened?" at times.

Caree Roles (Behaviors)

Carees tend to fall into certain patterns of behavior. They can be described as the following:

- **Resistant Caree:** It can seem that no matter what happens, this caree becomes upset about something. Reasons differ but are often tinged with a complaint or problem. Nothing is quite right, and they usually communicate their reason for worry or concern.
- **Helpless Caree:** Regardless of the caree's competency, they perceive themselves as helpless. They rarely come up with their own direction or are proactive in their care. They have a habit of asking for help. Inactivity is the norm.
- **Controlling Caree:** The caree demands or indirectly wants the attention of the caregiver. This behavior often masks a desire for love or affection. They may expect extensive phone contact. Once engaged, this caree will keep the caregiver tied up for long periods of time.
- **Grateful Caree:** One of the best ways of developing a healthy caregiver-caree relationship is through mutual appreciation and gratitude. In the grateful caree relationship, both the caree and the caregiver offer smiles, grateful hearts, and big hugs. This is an opportunity for the caregiver-caree to develop a loving relationship.

It is easy to understand the painful developments, as both caregiver and caree are experiencing loss and change. However, through honest communication, carees and their caregivers have an opportunity for developing a healthy relationship.

> "Please be patient with me.
> Sometimes when I am quiet, it's because
> I need to figure myself out. It's not because I don't
> want to talk. Sometimes there are no
> words for my thoughts."
> —*Kamla Bolanos*

ACCIDENTS AND LOSS OF MOBILITY

"Accidents happen. It's like a bomb that goes off
and pieces of shrapnel rip into the flesh of the family.
It's the families that need compassion."
—*James Belushi*

Surgery, as well as illness or accident, can cause loss of mobility. Regardless of the incident that results in lack of mobility, carees can feel helpless, slow, or disconnected. Being on crutches, in casts, or wheelchair-bound is an experience of powerlessness. Other people all seem to be "going by," and carees experience gut-wrenching feelings of being trapped and held back by their restraints.

After I broke my back falling down the stairs, I felt severely claustrophobic because the pain from my back made it impossible to move in any way. It was also very difficult to breathe. Both issues contributed to shallow breathing, which can itself become dangerous. The medical personnel kept me sedated with morphine much of the time to manage pain, but whenever I was awake I had trouble breathing.

When I graduated to a wheelchair, I very often felt invisible. But when someone looked at me and visited with me, I felt grateful. Being in a situation of learning to walk again and regaining full mobility was a powerful feeling of helplessness, which hurt and produced fear and depression. It's a sad place to be.

Sudden accidents or planned surgeries can lead to a lifestyle change, either temporary or sometimes permanent. It can happen at any age and stage. Mobility limitations may include the use of crutches, casts, boots, or wheelchairs. The loss of any part of our natural ability to move, to be fully functional, evokes powerful feelings and fears the mobile person can scarcely imagine. When a part of oneself is lost or impaired, whether it's a part of the body or a less obvious component, something essential is missing in our wholeness.

Carees know the feeling of tiredness, and sometimes-private terror, when they realize how and to what level their lives have changed. They may experience many disappointments. It's a lonely time. All want to return to the way it was before the accident, illness, or debilitation. What was normal is gone, and all will learn that there is no "going back to normal."

> *What was normal is gone, and all will learn that there is no "going back to normal."*

back to normal." A new normal will begin, which will shift and adjust many times.

DIAGNOSIS OF ILLNESS: ACUTE, CHRONIC, OR PROGRESSIVE

The diagnosis of an illness also brings with it the altering of what was normal to a new normal. Any number of illnesses can trigger loss—and a profound shift in ability. From diabetes, heart and pulmonary diseases, stroke, cancer, and multiple sclerosis to rheumatoid arthritis, chronic asthma, and bronchitis, Alzheimer's and Parkinson's diseases, and dementia, the change to the new normal may be either sudden or slow.

Depending upon the diagnosis, one is thrust into treatment plans and medication routines. But even more startling is the need to cancel the plans made in the "old normal" and to adjust

to behaviors that become part of the new normal. My own experience with heart disease, diabetes, and cancer has made me a
different person over the years as a caree. My experience with
my soul mate's illnesses of COPD, heart disease, C-difficile infec-
tion, life-threatening shingles, and frequent falls has changed my
normal many times as a caregiver.

Each of us over the years has felt many of these feelings for
various reasons:

- fear
- sadness
- fatigue
- diminution
- disappointment
- anxiety
- threatened
- internal ache
- humiliation
- anguish
- loneliness

"I don't know what it's like to not have deep emotions—
even when I feel nothing, I feel it completely."

—A. R. Asher

fear
sadness
tired
dismissed
disappointed
weary
anxiety
threat
internal ache
humiliation
anguish
loneliness
hurt

"Feelings are your guide. Trust them and learn to express them.
Be yourself and look to understand any crisis
you have been in or will be in."
—*Barbara Marciniak*

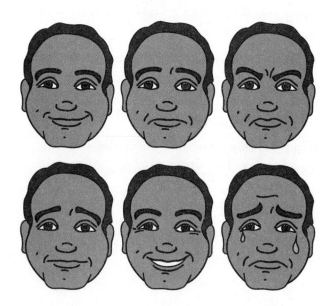

LOSS OF A MAJOR SENSE: TASTE AND SMELL

"The strongest people I've met have not been given an easier life.
They have learned to create strength and happiness from dark places."
—*Kristen Butler*

Most of us walk through life with our five major senses working well. Each sense is connected to a dedicated organ: eyes for sight, ears for hearing, tongue for taste, skin for touch, and nose for smell. To lose any sense requires learning to ask for help with that missing function. Both caree and caregiver are involved, for the loss of a sense changes many things for everyone affected.

My first experience of the loss of a sense was being close to someone who lost his sense of taste and smell. One day he was on a ladder, and then his life changed forever when he fell. He severed his olfactory nerve that resulted in the almost complete loss of two senses. It has taken years to learn the full extent of the consequence of that fall.

Taste and smell provide great comfort and pleasure. The tongue has about 9,000 taste buds. They are critical to taste and linked to smell, which protect us by alerting us to dangers such as smoke, gases, and spoiled food.

The loss of taste and smell is a massive blow, and he has handled it by using all his inner resources, especially acceptance and courage. It was primarily his journey and his loss. He doesn't expect me to do anything differently. Yet as his primary partner and caregiver, his loss changed my life as well. I cook differently, eat differently, and have developed attitudes and feelings of always keeping his loss at the top of my mind.

My soul mate adapted, drawing on parts of himself that he could work with, and doing so with courage and strength. He still has a minimal ability to taste on the tip of his tongue, allowing him to savor sweet and some sours. He can taste tomatoes. He does not enjoy bitter. As a caregiver, one of my roles has been to learn to cook many dishes that include tomatoes and get creative with sour foods while avoiding bitter or spicy flavors. Our family loves spicy, but we meet the challenge together, and we all make it work—a great comfort. We are closer because of this shared effort. We enjoy trying restaurants where everyone's needs can be met.

LOSS OF SIGHT

My grandma's loss of sight was a challenge for all the caregivers in her life. She was raised in the time before the availability of sight aids we now enjoy. Family members had always cared for her. For a time every year, she lived with each family member. In her later years, with her diabetes and loss of sight, she needed more care. Coupled with some of her caregivers developing their own physical and emotional health issues, it became a slippery slope for all. Her caregivers suffered great personal pain when they could no longer safely care for her. She eventually needed institutional care, which was hard for her to accept.

The loss of a grandparent is often the first major loss a family faces and can become a grand opportunity to learn how to grieve a human in a deep way. While the loss of a pet is a way to learn to grieve a death, the loss of a grandparent, and learning how to handle it in a healthy way, is part of a larger process and preparation for losing other family members (parents, siblings, partners, and cousins).

When I lost my grandmother, there were many lessons to learn. First, there was much pain from unresolved conflict that was left to her adult children. Some of that pain was passed down to my mother, and then to me when she died. Some was also passed down to my sister, which resulted in extra pain for her when she died.

My lessons from all of that learning about the effects of unresolved conflicts, unspoken feelings and thoughts, avoided decision-making, and unmet expectations has helped me make many different choices about my eventual death. I hope that the plans that I have put in place will make it easier for my children and grandchildren to go on in their lives with less pain than my grandmother's unresolved conflict passed on to her children upon her death.

In many other different ways, my grandmother's death was a healing time and a role model that I would like to use to plan my death. She was very close to her grandchildren and she taught me many lessons in life and at death about how to be a grandma. I hope I have passed on that part of her legacy.

For those of you who still have the chance, connect with your grandparents if that is possible. Learn whatever lessons you can learn and maybe offer whatever you can in regard to their care needs right now. It can be a rich experience.

HEARING LOSS:
AMERICA'S SILENT AND GROWING EPIDEMIC

Loss of hearing is often not seen as the serious issue it is. Confusion exists regarding the natural hearing loss that can come with aging. Of course, serious conditions can result in major hearing loss, which can be subtle and emerge slowly or significant and occur suddenly.

Hearing loss affects more than 48 million Americans, according to the Hearing Loss Association of America. It may also increase the risk of cognitive problems and even dementia. By the time Americans reach their seventies, two-thirds have hearing loss. About one in three adults ages sixty-five to seventy-four have hearing loss, and almost half of people older than seventy-five have trouble hearing, according to the U.S. National Institutes of Health.

"The general perception is that hearing loss is a relatively inconsequential part of aging," says Frank Lin, an otologist and epidemiologist at Johns Hopkins University in Baltimore. Multiple studies he has led have shown that hearing loss appears to speed up age-related cognitive decline. Lin notes, however, that simply being at increased risk does not mean a person is certain to develop dementia. If ongoing research confirms the connection between hearing loss and dementia, it raises the possibility that treating hearing loss more aggressively could help stave off cognitive decline and dementia.

At any age, frustration and fear can bubble up for the person experiencing hearing loss. Likewise, frustration, fear, loss, and anger occur in those near to the person who is suffering with hearing loss. In early stages of gradual hearing loss, no one knows for sure what is happening. Incomplete hearing can lead to misunderstandings and hurt feelings. Doesn't the other person understand me?

Feelings run through many stages with the major loss of one of the senses. Hearing loss, as well as loss of other senses, must be grieved. Once the loss is fully realized, a great deal of pain is experienced not only by the one who has lost hearing but also by those nearest to the person. No one accepts and gets used to living with hearing loss overnight. It is sometimes years before the full extent of the loss is known and faced.

At first, in the myriad of losses, hearing doesn't seem like a major one, such as sight or the ability to walk. However, one learns quickly that it is a major loss that can be life threatening.

My first experience as a "hearing loss caregiver" occurred when my much younger sister suffered from tinnitus. My first response was, "It can't be as serious as she tells me." I went through hours of listening about her agony. I attempted to give her solace, but I always failed.

Understanding the extent of the pain that the condition can inflict came when I was walking around the nurses' stations at the Mayo Clinic in Rochester, Minnesota, with my sister, who said, "I would rather die than ever face tinnitus again. It drove me crazy and has cost me. I would choose hospice and get relief before I would face that condition again." As it turned out, my sister developed a fast-moving cancer, and she died three months later.

Other experiences with good friends who have begun to have hearing loss have helped me learn to recognize the symptoms:

- leaning in to the conversation to hear
- responding with an inappropriate answer
- getting quieter when not following a conversation
- speaking louder and louder and appearing to be controlling—when coupled with a person with strong opinions, that person gets increasingly harder to be around
- feelings of anxiety because of "not hearing" and not knowing the consequences of "not hearing"
- seeming more confused when one cannot pick up the signals—without a reality check, confusion is guaranteed
- feelings of isolation
- anger in relationships over misunderstandings, commitments, and what feels like lack of love and support

In Case of Significant Hearing Loss

If hearing loss is significant, the person experiencing it needs to:

- give up driving; it's not safe to drive if one cannot hear;
- agree to reach out for help and ask for help;
- learn to accept loss of hearing as a major disability;
- move beyond denial to acceptance and lifestyle adjustment;
- find other ways to contribute—find purpose in the new quieter world;
- celebrate that he or she has an internal sensor of noise and move into another kind of acceptance; and
- learn to ask for every technology for help.

Someone else is most often the first to notice hearing loss. It is a signal for a necessary change in attitude and lifestyle. It does not define anyone.

How to Help the Person Experiencing Hearing Loss

If any of the symptoms of hearing loss is present, take the following actions:

- Face the person when you speak. Get used to looking them "right in the eye."
- Speak as loudly and as distinctly that feels comfortable.
- Learn to repeat as needed; this requires patience and acceptance.
- Ask questions if not communicating.
- Give the benefit of whether it's "resistance" or "inability."
- Always be kind; it's frustrating for all.
- Reduce background noise from TVs, dishwashers, or other sources.
- Say their name before starting to talk.
- Speak more slowly and stay calm.
- Choose only quiet restaurants and avoid places that have a lot of echo.
- Help the person choose supportive friends.

LOSS OF TOUCH

The sense of touch is active within our bodies at all times. It is what pulls us back from a hot stove, helps us walk over a rocky surface, and protects us by aiding our balance. This huge network of nerve endings, known as the sensory system, enables us to know whether we are hot or cold, whether something is rough or smooth, or if we feel itchy or are in pain. It is basically what helps develop and affects all our other senses.

MANAGING THE IMPACT OF SENSORY LOSS

Senses provide valuable information; therefore, when any of our senses are less sharp, a caregiver can provide some of the sensory input that's missing. We are not helpless in the face of sensory loss. We can wear glasses or undergo surgery and therapies to reduce the impact of cataracts, glaucoma, macular degeneration, and retinopathy. We can adapt to hearing loss with the help of group conversations, interpretations, devices, surgeries, and environmental settings. But most important of all is our emotional response.

When we experience loss of sensory capacity through accident, age, or illness, anger can become a major emotion in the caregiver-caree relationship. The closer the relationship, the deeper the anger can be. What is intentional on the part of the caree and what is "pure inability"? It can become a war. As the sensory loss deepens, eventually fear takes hold. "What is happening?" Finally, acceptance comes. How do we find the new normal as the losses grow deeper?

> "First you cry and then you do the laundry."
> —*Anonymous*

When we reach emotional bottom, it can feel very lonely, very desperate, and always overwhelming. Then you move on. What else is there to do? My friend who is losing her hearing is one of the most loving people I know. At first, she denied her hearing loss because of pride and age. She has beautiful hair, so her hearing aids do not show. After all, she is vivacious, smart, and sassy. Her love life is strong, and she would give you the blouse off her back. Yet her struggle to stay involved is evident. She often isolates.

"But hearing loss doesn't only affect older people.
The World Health Organization estimated that 1.1 billion teenagers and
young adults are at risk of hearing loss. And that number is increasing.
Boomers had their rock concerts, and millennials have their ear buds.
So the impact of hearing damage will likely grow."
—*AARP Bulletin, May 2018*

"I don't believe in aging. I believe in forever altering one's aspect to the sun."
—*Virginia Woolf*

SPECIAL NEEDS: SOME HAVE MORE THAN OTHERS

"When the unthinkable happens, the lighthouse is hope.
Once we choose hope, everything is possible."
—*Christopher Reeve*

Some people are born with developmental mental or physical needs that will last a lifetime, and for whom a professionally paid or family caregiver has taken on the responsibility of meeting those needs. In this situation, agencies, lawyers, hands-on caregivers, group homes, and decision makers all become part of the caregiving team, because it takes a whole team of individuals to provide that level of sustained care.

"You either get bitter or you get better. It's that simple.
You either take what has been dealt to you and allow it to make
you a better person, or you allow it to tear you down.
The voice does not belong to fate; it belongs to you."
—*Josh Shipp*

LONG-DISTANCE CARING

"Regret for the things we have done will be tempered by time.
It is regret for the things we did not do that is inconsolable."
—*Sydney J. Harris*

In our current mobile way of life, the caregiver and the caree often live some distance apart. The situation has spawned new industries of helping from a distance. Food delivery, financial aid, and coordinating care become a new way of replacing hands-on care.

Care from a distance also exposes feelings of pain within family systems, and much negotiating will need to take place between those who provide day-to-day care and those who make that care possible by planning, assuming cost, and making decisions.

It is best when there is ongoing communication about the caree from both the hands-on caregivers and the long distant providers of care. They are both caregivers in different ways. In some families, these negotiations are very cordial and a win-win for everyone. Often, however, there is discord and disagreement between the day-to-day people and the distant family members. And sometimes families grow apart and are not involved at all.

Every happy and satisfied family often provides caregiving in the same ways, with communication, appreciation and care for the caree—and caregivers. Every family that hurts often hurts in the same way, with judgment, rigidity, righteousness, and control. Every family system is different.

"Distance gives us a reason to love harder."
—*Jane Clark*

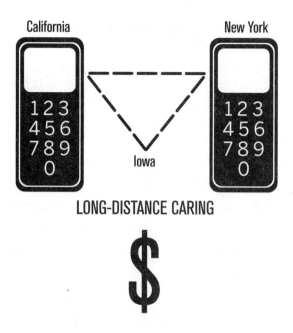

LONG-DISTANCE CARING

FINANCIAL CAREGIVING

"To care for those who once cared for us
is one of the highest honors."
—*Tia Walker*

Finances in connection with caregiving are serious issues for all ages. The young have trouble getting jobs that offer health insurance, until they have careers of their own. Some, to a certain age, are on their parents' medical insurance plan. However, too often, young people are uninsured and need financial help for a chronic condition.

Some retirees receive a monthly pension. Many elderly people collect Social Security benefits. Depending on political and economic shifts, Social Security and Medicare could be at risk.

Financial caregiving for every age is often lacking. While this subject is too big and complex to cover in this book, the fact is that some people have health insurance and many go without it. Suffice it to say that every mature person has a responsibility to learn about finances, self-care, and preparing for the day when he or she might need care or become a caregiver. Alice Walker helps us come to grips with the new normal in financial caregiving when she tells us: "I try to teach my heart to want nothing it can't have."

MENTORS AND HEROES AS CAREGIVERS

"We can see further by standing on the shoulders of giants."
—Isaac Newton

I believe that some people are caregivers by virtue of the example and inspiration they give others. They can be heroes known around the world or mentors who quietly lead others by living their lives with grace despite severe challenges. I have named a few such heroes and mentors who have inspired me.

HELEN KELLER

An American author and political activist, Helen Keller was left both deaf and blind when she contracted an illness, likely scarlet fever, when she was only nineteen months old. She became known around the world for being outspoken and brave. Keller was the first deaf-blind person to earn a Bachelor of Arts degree in the United States. She wrote many books and essays, and inspired many others with her courage. Highly ambitious, Keller beat the heavy odds

against her success and devoted her life to helping others. Anne
Sullivan, her famous teacher, was also a caregiver to Helen and, as
the movie title about her life aptly stated, a miracle worker. Anne
stayed with her from the time she was twenty until she died.

> "Life is either a daring adventure or nothing."
> —*Helen Keller*

STEPHEN HAWKING

A highly educated English theoretical physicist and author,
Stephen Hawking had a rare, early onset, slow-progressing form
of amyotrophic lateral sclerosis (ALS). Hawking slowly became
paralyzed but rose to become the Director of Research for Theoretical Cosmology at the University of Cambridge before his death.
Married with children despite the disease, he was known for his
brilliance, intelligence, and sense of humor. Hawking inspired
millions with his wonderful outlook on life.

> "However difficult life may seem, there is always something you can do,
> and succeed at. It matters that you don't just give up."
> —*Stephen Hawking*

DEBORAH M. HAZELTON

It was my privilege to know Deborah Hazelton, known to her
friends as Debbie. She and I were both lucky enough to be authors
for pioneering articles and books published by *U.S. Journal* and
Health Communications, the publisher of this book. One time when
I was in Florida, Debbie invited me to her home. She said she lived
within walking distance. Debbie was blind, and I wasn't sure exactly

where she lived. When I agreed to go with her, she said, "Let's go." Debbie then led me to her house and into the most exciting and incredible workspace, where she had authored her book, an affirmation work titled *The Courage to See*. That book became part of my daily meditation routine, as her words gave me hope, courage, and inspiration. Debbie autographed my copy of her book with her name and her dog's paw print.

> "It takes courage to grow up and become who you really are."
> —*E. E. Cummings*

MICHAEL J. FOX

For years, Michael J. Fox gave me laughter and joy through his role of Alex on *Family Ties*. As a mom with a son who had many of Alex's traits, I related to that TV show. Michael continues to inspire as a role model. He is a successful actor, author, producer, and activist, and has remained joy-filled and courageous while facing his own diagnosis of Parkinson's disease. He gives hope to individuals, families, and all who face the same situation. We keep one of his quotes on a mirror at home to read daily.

> "I don't have a choice of whether or not I have Parkinson's, but surrounding that non-choice are a million other choices that I can make."
> —*Michael J. Fox*

ALAN ALDA

Known around the world, Alan Alda noticed his hand shaking while filming his new TV show. He chose to publicly announce his diagnosis of Parkinson's disease. Rather than a press release of a sad story about his disease, he wanted everyone to know his is not a sad story. For him, life is as good as it ever was.

> "(My diagnosis) has not changed my life at all.
> I've had a richer life than I've had up until now."
> —*Alan Alda*

While I have many stories of caregivers and carees who have influenced my life, I will close this section with a story of Mary Olson, my maternal grandmother, who was both a caregiver and a caree for much of her eighty-six years.

> "She made broken look beautiful and strong look invincible.
> She walked with the universe on her shoulders and
> made it look like a pair of wings."
> —*Ariana Dancu*

MARY OLSON

I have framed my grandmother's bankbook from the 1930s and 1940s. She never had more than $325.00 at any one time in her almost nine decades of life. However, Mary managed to successfully raise four children, two of them orphans whom she took in, while working full time in the local café as the primary cook. In high school, my girlfriends and I would visit her and wait tables. Mary turned out twenty-one kinds of donuts long before donut shops were popular. She was also caregiver of my grandfather, who suffered with a somewhat debilitating rheumatoid arthritis.

Mary always dressed up and wore a brooch on her dress (I still wear two of them). She had a smile and hug for everyone. She suffered from diabetes, with treatment better at some times than others, and eventually lost her sight to the illness.

Mary planned her funeral the week before she died. She instructed the family priest to ask the family to heal disagreements among them before they were offered communion—and they did. Mary asked for her nineteen grandchildren to file up to her casket and put something in that she would take with her into eternity. She received everything from a garden hoe and a bottle of Mogen David wine to a bottle of Blue Waltz perfume. Mary was an amazing example of a woman with grit, courage, and personality as both caregiver and caree. I am proud to be her granddaughter.

> "Find people who challenge and inspire you, spend time with them and it will change your life."
> —Amy Poehler

They reframed their challenges as opportunities for bringing something positive into their lives—or into the lives of others.

All these hero and mentor caregivers had one thing in common in overcoming the obstacles they faced: reframing. They reframed their challenges as opportunities for bringing something positive into their lives—or into the lives of others.

Reframing is a limitless tool for looking at a situation from more than one perspective. The payoff is a change of outlook and attitude, which goes a long way toward healing and happiness. Learning to look at the upside of downside happenings is a thread that will run through the rest of this book. Reframing suggests that carees and caregivers have more in common than has been previously acknowledged.

In my office at home stands a stuffed giraffe. He sits about three feet high and stares at me with deep piercing eyes. When lying in my bed in rehab, home felt very distant to me. I asked my family to bring me my giraffe. She has sat and stared at me whenever I write, bringing me great comfort. Seeing him in rehab brought me closer to home, which brought me great joy. You might note that sometimes I refer to my giraffe as "he" and sometimes as "she." I could not think of a good name because I didn't know if the giraffe is a he or a she, which piqued my curiosity. When people would stop by my room, they noticed her and asked about the name. At that moment, an idea for a contest formed.

I asked everyone—nurses, dining room attendants, housecleaners, mail carriers, and family members—how to tell a male giraffe from a female. No one knew. As soon as I could sit, I went online but found no answer. The quest generated lots of interest, however, and became a point of conversation. The next step was to start a contest to name my giraffe. The invite went out to all at the rehab facility, and then I included it in an e-mail and sent it to my friends. I asked everyone to send me names.

The hours flew by while I was in the rehab as my focus was somewhere other than my painful situation. Family and friends got involved, and we had more to talk about than how they or I was feeling. My giraffe played a role in my progress. I sat up, stood up, and eventually took small steps. When I graduated to walking around the building with a walker and could go up and down three steps, I was finally ready to go home.

The winning name in the contest was Heshe (pronounced *he-she*). The consensus was that the name was enough. No one needed to know her gender. It was not as important as finding an identity. At that time, with a simple reframe, pain turned to hope, isolation turned to community, and weakness turned to strength. Heshe continues to live in my office.

Being a caree is hard. Some kind of loss is always involved—physical, mental, and/or emotional. It is hard work on every level. But when carees find a way to reframe their situations, to gain a new perspective, they can bring about positive change for themselves—and for others.

In the next chapter, we'll see the tremendous toll caregiving can take on the caregiver—and what they can do to protect themselves from burnout.

BURNED OUT:
IS THIS ALL THERE IS?

*When long-term exhaustion meets
diminished interest.*

—Anonymous

If you have been caregiving too much for too long, the signs become clear. You do any one or more of the following:

- go to bed and pull up the covers
- isolate
- resist connection with others
- cut people out of your life
- "visit" most of your friends on a screen
- sleep poorly and irregularly
- surf store websites or shop on Amazon

- let your appearance go
- develop poor eating habits
- gain too many pounds
- look for someone to blame
- stop having fun
- sit at the computer too long
- become accident prone
- develop prescription pill dependency
- experience financial problems
- become unable to make decisions
- get depressed
- develop a smoking or vaping dependency

I CAN'T DO IT ANYMORE!

Any of these behaviors are usually a cover for anger, guilt, hurt, grief, shame, fear, and many other feelings. Not until those emotions are named, felt, and then expressed will the behaviors have any chance to heal. Feelings of the caregiver bounce up and down all the time—in direct and indirect relationship to their caree, and in relation to how they are taking care of themselves.

GUILT

"If you stumble, make it part of the dance."
—*Anonymous*

It is natural and normal to feel some kind of guilt during a caregiving journey. Remember that none of us is perfect; we will all have regrets and make mistakes. However, be kind to yourself and be gentle with your own self-love. It seems like caregivers feel they never do enough or in the right way.

ANGER

"Feelings are something you have—not something you are."
—*Shannon L. Alder*

Anger comes so easily in the form of frustration, disappointment, and irritation. The signs of anger will be high and on frequent display during caregiving. Remember that carees are often upset with themselves, and it's easier to lash out at a caregiver than to feel all the pain he or she is naturally experiencing.

Double anger is a term I use when the caregiver gets upset and angry over little and big things and then lashes out at the caree. The relentlessness of being let down, dealing with memory problems, or feeling neglected is sometimes just "too much," and there is an explosion of feeling. The behavior then swings back and forth, and the anger becomes exaggerated, often including criticism and blame. Caregivers can say hurtful things that trigger shame within themselves. They become someone they don't like. It's a vicious circle and everyone suffers. The original incident gets lost in the ongoing hurt. This is double anger.

Behavior anger is not spoken but rather acted out. This behavior is usually directed at someone the caregiver is angry with but they are afraid to put the anger into words. Whenever anger is not expressed in a healthy way, it leads to either depression or inappropriate behavior. The most common way anger shows up is in passive-aggressive behavior patterns, such as the following:

- chronic lateness
- the silent treatment
- criticism
- judging
- blaming
- controlling (directly or indirectly)

The situation cannot and will not change until the anger is recognized and appropriately expressed. In this situation, social

A good friend told me, "In the space between the bitter and the sweet are the tears."

services or a counselor or a support group can be of great help. Anger can lead to a devastating feeling or become a guide to behavior change. A good friend told me, "In the space between the bitter and the sweet are the tears." Both the person being cared for and the person giving care find the tears.

SHAME

"Each patient carries his own doctor inside him."
—*Norman Cousins*

Shame is all about not feeling good enough. Most caregivers picture themselves as loving, caring, nurturing, patient, and understanding of the caree but do not feel the same way toward themselves. They tend to be critical, at times downright mean, impatient, and lost. All of it is true. That is how caregiving is: relentless, constant, unforgiving, and controlling. It's a hard and painful place to be. Many times, both the caree and the caregiver do not feel good about themselves at all. It is a tough road to walk.

FEAR

"You wake up each morning to fight the same demons that left you tired the night before, and that, my love, is bravery."
—*Anonymous*

Fear is not knowing what comes next. Living in fear can leave the caregiver in a state of emergency alert or hypervigilance, always waiting for the next shoe to drop. Fear leads to massive fatigue. During the overwork and stress, the caregiver is a prime candidate for stress-related illnesses or conditions, including diabetes, chronic fatigue, insomnia, and high blood pressure. Unrelieved stress can also make a caregiver more accident prone.

GRIEF

"Courage does not always roar. Sometimes, courage is the quiet voice
at the end of the day saying, 'I will try again tomorrow.'"
—*Mary Anne Radmacher*

Caregivers sometimes don't recognize that they are in grief along with the caree. Much has been written about the grief of one who is losing independence, whether it is physical, emotional, mental, or a combination of losses. Not as much has been said about the caregiver who is also feeling grief over losing the caree.

In a professional relationship, the feelings of sadness and constant loss are wearing. To avoid feeling inner emptiness, the caregiver needs time and space to refill his or her reserve. When caring for someone we love, our grief can be enormous, and many of us really don't want to feel the power of the loss. We often go into denial, refusing to see or accept obvious changes and self-defeating behaviors. It becomes easier "not to talk" about this grief. But it's important to be brave enough to talk.

Signs and Complications of Serious Burnout

The five areas most affected by serious burnout are the following:

1. **Stress Eating**
   - trying multiple diets, rarely sticking to one
   - preoccupation with food and fast food
   - often takeout—using food as a medication

- a million recipes available, a freezer full of food, but choosing a takeout hamburger

2. **Running Around and Running Away**
   - rarely sitting still and hurting through the loss of self
   - busy, busy, and busier

3. **Preoccupation with Projects**
   - remodeling
   - finding certain clothes
   - doing a hobby
   - cleaning
   - decluttering
   - decorating
   - downsizing
   - collecting, etc.

4. **Relationship Issues**
   - difficulty focusing on and remaining honest and authentic—overly available or overly private
   - responding to projected feelings of others
   - attaching to needy people

5. **Technology Dependence**
   - feeling uncomfortable with the responsibility of face-to-face connection
   - becoming dependent on phone, texting, and computer—often dependent on more than one device

When burnout reaches this level of seriousness, expect complications, which most often show up in the following ways:

1. **Sleep issues:** It becomes hard to "turn off" and fall asleep. It's also hard to stay awake because you face the morning already tired.
2. **Physical symptoms:** In addition to weight gain, parts of the body begin to break down from carrying too much

weight. It's harder to exercise, more weight is gained, and a vicious cycle begins. Physical breakdown includes high blood pressure, muscle strain, and irritability.

3. **Depression:** This begins with feelings of persistent pessimism and worry, then an increase of negative self-talk, repetitive thoughts, and difficulty concentrating or making decisions. An estimated 20 million adults in the United States suffer from depression. Caregiver-related depression is higher among those caring for a person with dementia or a spousal caregiver whose partner has died, according to the *Caregiver Helpbook*.

4. **Discontent:** High stress levels increase the risk of chronic illness, anxiety, or problems of behavioral control. Care-givers become quick to pronounce opinion and to criticize. It's hard to be around a controlling or discontented person.

MAGICAL THINKING

"The world is entirely magical; the only illusion is that it isn't."
—Lydia Andal

Magical thinking is thinking problems will be resolved when

- the caree gets "back to normal," and then the caregiver can get back to normal;
- caregiver issues, which are due to an outside force, will be resolved. One is unwilling to look at one's own role in the process of burnout;
- the caregiver refuses to ask for help. The caregiver says, "I can take care of this myself. I do not need outside help or a

support group." Rule of thumb: people with good impulse control and connection to themselves and the world are quick to ask for outside help. People who suffer from "I can handle my stress myself" usually have symptoms that branch out and multiply; and

- the desire for privacy rules. The caregiver says, "I'm a really private person and do not want outside people knowing my business. My business is private and I can control it."

HOW TO ASK FOR HELP

> "Be strong enough to stand alone, smart enough to know when
> you need help, and brave enough to ask for it."
> —*Ziad K. Abdelnour*

One would think that caregivers are the first people who know the value of outside help. In my counseling agency, a successful organization that has helped and continues to help millions of people, I usually hire professionals who were in some kind of professional care themselves and/or were involved in self-help support groups. Their experience aids their understanding and compassion of all that is involved in caregiving. Many sources of help are available:

- inpatient and outpatient residential care programs
- psychologists
- clinical social workers
- marriage and family therapists
- support groups for addiction, eating disorders, gambling, and drug dependency

Each person must find a way to enlist personal or group help, but the first step is asking where, who, and how. The second step is to take action. Burnout is a one-way street until an intervention occurs. The intervention, self-initiated or accomplished with the help of others, happens when people hit bottom and seek, or are given, help. Without outside care, too often the result is one of the following:

- a crash and burn
- an accident
- a self-destructive lifestyle—addiction, obesity, health problems

It's been said that caregiving is often the final walk you take with someone you love. Do everything you can to enjoy the journey.

Caregiving is one of the most difficult jobs on this earth and yet provides the greatest personal growth and joy. It's been said that caregiving is often the final walk you take with someone you love. Do everything you can to enjoy the journey.

"The amount of good luck coming your way
depends on your willingness to act."
—Barbara Sher

WHEN A CAREGIVER'S AND A CAREE'S PATHS CROSS

"Don't be the reason someone feels insecure. Be the reason someone
feels seen, heard and supported by the whole universe."
—Cleo Wade

Many ways are available for the caregiver and caree to connect, listen to each other, and work through feelings and situations, but these conversations do not take place as often as they should. As we further break down the problems and energy drains, it is beneficial to explore specific tools that may help relieve burnout.

Big questions should be explored through frequent and realistic conversations about the issues that arise within the caregiver-caree relationship. Burnout is likely to happen when families avoid or do not discuss these issues.

Key Issues to Discuss in the Caregiving Family

1. When does the caree stop driving, and how do all involved respond to challenges of transportation?
2. When and how to avoid crowds—for those with weakened immune systems—and still avoid loneliness?
3. How can all the caregivers in a family contribute to the well-being of the caree to prevent the burden from falling on just one or two people?
4. Who is on the caregiving team, and how is responsibility divided so that no one person bears it all?
5. Is the family open to receiving comments and input from outside the family in order to lower stress and increase productivity?
6. When does downsizing take place?
7. How does that downsizing affect members in the extended family?
8. When are grandparents able and unable to help with grandchildren?
9. What are the opinions and attitudes of each family member, and how are they shared?
10. Who will take what responsibility at the time of death of the caree in the family?
11. Has someone helped the caregiver/caree through all the required legal paperwork?
12. How can the family plan a "no regret" end of life?
13. Are financial legacies finished?
14. Are emotional and psychological legacies transmitted?

15. Will the family cherish this "changing" time, or will they wish they had done it differently?

Once the caree, the caregiver, and the family address these issues, they've created a family system that will likely allow them to face all that is to come in the natural process of life and death. The last stage of life can then be fueled by joy.

HOPE IS BORN

"Every storm in your life is followed by a rainbow."
—*Doreen Virtue*

Burnout in most endeavors usually means it's time for reframing, making choices, and accepting and developing a new normal. It's time to change the behavior that has led to the multiple feelings of depression and exhaustion. Once burnout begins to be felt, a blanket feeling of confusion, fog, and emptiness ensues. The caregiver feels it and others can see it. If some part of your life isn't working well, it is good to look inside and find the source, repair what you can, then return to a state of relative harmony, inner peace, and self-acceptance.

HEALTHY SEPARATION AND ACCEPTANCE

*We must let go of the life we have planned, so as
to accept the one that is waiting for us.*

—Joseph Campbell

Separating the caree from his or her illness is critical. Each situation has to be weighed individually and carefully. Some illnesses are intertwined, and it's very hard, and sometimes dangerous, to combine them.

For example, your caree may have had a lifelong habit of leaving things undone—simple things such as not emptying the dishwasher, or replacing the empty roll of toilet with a new one—familiar failings but no less annoying. Add to this habit a diagnosis of dementia. Now the habit—old business—may get bound up with the new illness. Are they forgetting because they're just forgetting? Or does the presence of dementia add a new layer to the situation so that the person just can't help it? It's a slippery slope. It's in these times when it's important that the family has already established good communication systems.

Now the habit—old business—may get bound up with the new illness. Are they forgetting because they're just forgetting? Or does the presence of dementia add a new layer to the situation so that the person just can't help it? It's a slippery slope.

Where possible, it's best to separate behavior from the value of the person. It's okay and quite appropriate to feel frustration, anger, and even disgust with someone who is behaving badly—controlling, confusing, and/or inept. If their illness is keeping them from "normal expected responses" and causing caretakers or family members extra stress and constraints or restraints on their time, hurt feelings will go all the way around.

The first separation is realizing that the person progressing in an illness—especially illnesses that involve the thinking process—is changing. The caregiving responsibility is to do the best one can to continue to care and respect the person they are dealing with. At the same time, one needs to accept and appropriately express his or her feelings about the behavior that goes with this illness. It becomes important at many different levels to set boundaries, which is perfectly normal and necessary. It is also the caregiver's responsibility to find ways to share his or her frustrations, disappointments, and anger.

SETTING PRACTICAL BOUNDARIES

1. SURRENDERING KEYS TO THE CAR

Most spousal caregivers hope that the caree will willingly give up the keys to the car when they are clearly no longer able to drive safely. If the caree refuses, someone—usually the spouse or the caregiver team—has to take them away. This is tricky ground to negotiate, for many painful issues arise. When does one stop driving? The clear answer is when someone is dangerous to self or others. That could be at any age. I experienced two accidents in 2017—both while in recovery and sitting in a parked car in a handicap signed area. One was serious and involved $10,000 worth of damage. The other was minor, but did damage my car. Both times an elderly person who should not have been driving hit me.

It's Not Just About Age

Giving up the car keys is not just about age. It's about skill and attentiveness. If someone cannot leave their phone alone in the car, they should not be driving (lack of focus). Phone-related accidents are common (from fender benders to fatal accidents). The National Highway Traffic Safety Administration (NHTSA) reports that in 2015, "distracted drivers" killed 3,477 people. In addition, 391,000 were injured and 551 non-occupants—bicyclists and pedestrians—were killed.

2. RIDING WITH AN IMPAIRED CAREE DRIVER

No matter what the reason—alcohol, medication, distraction, or aging—caregivers have the responsibility of not letting anyone ride with an impaired caree driver—just as parents are responsible not to let their children ride with any impaired driver.

3. ACKNOWLEDGING THE NEED FOR SLEEP

When carees and caregivers live together, the need for regular sleep is especially important. Neither will function in a healthy way without it; it's a common and persistent problem. Snoring and noisy devices that provide oxygen to manage sleep apnea, such as CPAP machines, can disturb sleep, as can bladder issues that require multiple nightly bathroom visits. Both are major sleep robbers and add to caregiver stress.

Few situations are as variable as sleep patterns. As some develop dementia or cognitive issues, they also start getting insomnia and are up at all hours of the night. Others who may be experiencing other physical or mental illness such as heart disease, depression, or weakened immune systems choose to sleep much of the time. Each person is different and caregiving needs to adjust to how the caree is responding to the need for sleep. If the caree-caregiver relationship is between spouses, both need to discuss the problem and negotiate solutions to their sleep needs.

4. CREATING PRIVATE SPACE IN A SHARED HOME OR AN APARTMENT

Whether just two or many family members live in the same home—and sometimes up to three generations share the same space—multiple issues will arise that need to be discussed and negotiated, including the following:

- sound from the TV and radio, and music style
- cooking styles
- sleeping times
- privacy and alone time

Illnesses such as Alzheimer's disease, Parkinson's disease, and dementia come with issues that become hard to manage and to hold someone accountable. The caree's ability to be accountable is somewhat limited.

When many people live in the same home, it is helpful for each person to claim a few places in the home that are their *private spaces*. It may be a room in a larger house, a corner in a smaller house, or a TV spot (with earphones), bedroom space, and even certain chairs for each person in the home. In difficult situations, a locked drawer or desk and files provide some privacy. Separate phones are very important. Each household and the specific needs of its members need to be addressed on an individual basis.

Let me offer an example of dealing with the issue of space and possessions—first with irritation, then with compassion, and eventually with humor.

My soul mate, my caree, surrounds himself with paper, which drives me to tears sometimes with all the extra photos, papers, and documents he has in boxes stashed everywhere. One day, after my complaining about it, he threw much of it away. Since ridding himself of so much, he had many regrets, for he has lost so much of his memory. Little did he know that I went to the trash and brought much of it back into the house. Over time I made a 500-page scrapbook. Now he often walks down his "memory lane" with his scrapbook. I'm so glad I retrieved as much as I did. He now talks about the scrapbook he put together.

One day, I went through some of my selected papers that I had stored in a banker's box I intended to get to "someday." The box was full, but I got to work sorting. When I got down about two inches, I found all of "his" papers he had hidden under mine, knowing they would be safe there. Space can be carved out almost anywhere. Trips to a memory care center can be curtailed or avoided if carees are incorporated into a way of life that allows privacy to all. If the person needing care cannot give or take privacy, then the time may come for twenty-four-hour management or a full-time memory care solution.

Perhaps we all carry many of our stories on photos and papers, and they are more important than we thought. Photos are great memory triggers. There are still many who don't have or store photos on their cell phones or computers, or don't regularly use these devices. When saving photos for them, it's important to print out photos, make notes on the back, and put them in a scrapbook, or at least in a box. So many family members have told me about the boxes of photos their parents have that mean a great deal to the caree, but no one in the family knows the who, what, when, or where details of the photos. Upon dementia or death, the boxes simply get thrown away, along with years of history and recording.

> "It is not our differences that divide us. It is our inability to recognize, accept and celebrate those differences."
> —Audre Lorde

CHOOSING TO LOVE AND CARE

"You have to fight through some bad days to earn the best days of your life."
—*Inspired Living Affirmation*

Once you've separated the person from the illness, a cloud lifts and you sense a reconnection with the heart and soul of the person whom you love and care for. The struggle of illness, as well as the victories, is shared between the caree and those who care about him or her.

Once you've separated the person from the illness, a cloud lifts and you sense a reconnection with the heart and soul of the person whom you love and care for.

There is a release of energy and focus when meeting the needs of the illness while enjoying the person. Everyone gets to be truly the best "me" they can be.

Once this internal separation has been made, acceptance and courage along with hope and healing all begin to happen, and wisdom flourishes. Life is much richer for both the caregiver and the caree. Joy and inner peace become part of the situation. I think Claire Danes best described my experience with the acceptance of illness and separating the person from the illness—and how it allows me to plan my life around the challenges the illness has presented—when she said, "People confuse fame with validation or love. But fame is not the reward. The reward is getting fulfillment out of doing the thing you love." Life itself then becomes the goal, not the busyness of activity while trying to seek meaning in life.

"Everyone has his own specific vocation or mission in life:
everyone must carry out a concrete assignment that demands fulfillment.
Therein he cannot be replaced, nor can his life be repeated.
Thus, everyone's task is unique as is his specific
opportunity to implement it."
—*Viktor E. Frankl*

PUTTING TOGETHER THE TOOLBOX

Even the simplest tools can empower
people to do great things.

—Biz Stone

When something around the house is broken, you reach into your toolbox for the right tool to make the repair. Occasionally, you add special tools for special tasks. Both carees and caregivers need a toolbox.

In studying basic needs of humans, everyone from the psychologist Abraham Maslow to motivational speaker and coach Tony Robbins has a numbered list of basic human needs. We will devise our own for this book. Once we understand the nature of our needs, we will know what tools to have available in our toolbox. Although we're all aware of our simple basic needs, paying attention to them in a simple, daily, useful way is a whole different story.

Imagine each person's toolbox has three sections: basic needs, ongoing needs, and thriving needs. Then begin to gather tools to meet the needs in each of the sections:

Section 1. Caregiver and Caree Basic Needs

- food
- water
- shelter
- sleep
- air

Section 2. Caregiver and Caree Ongoing Needs

- connection
- transportation
- safety
- resilience

Section 3. Caregiver and Caree Thriving Needs

- purpose
- self-respect
- relief
- time
- savoring

"The art of appreciation begins with self-appreciation."
—*Amit Abraham*

As we begin to assemble our toolboxes, let's start with the following frame of mind:

- Give yourself credit for everything you do that is right.
- Count yourself as kind if you give smiles several times a day.
- Erase all guilt from each moment or tool for self-care while you care for someone else.
- Feel good about yourself in your private memory bank; you are more than a caregiver or a caree.

General principles for caregiving

- Commit to smaller ideas and tasks.
- Do not worry about success or failure; this is all about trying out new ways of doing things.
- Start with three suggestions:

    1. Start fresh from this moment on (inside and outside). The past is no longer in charge; you are.
    2. Trust in something beyond "I can do this myself."
    3. Keep in mind your well-being and that of those around you.

SECTION 1: CAREGIVER AND CAREE BASIC NEEDS

FOOD: FACING BEING OVERWEIGHT AND MAKING FOOD MAGIC HAPPEN

"In my food world there is no fear and guilt,
only joy and balance."
—*Ellie Krieger*

Meals are one of the most constant needs of a caree and care-giver—and one of the most difficult to manage. The added stress of caregiving can throw off a regular rhythm for meal planning, shopping, meal prep, and mealtimes. Problems can easily crop up: Eating too much of the wrong kinds of foods. Eating to meet emotional needs. Food dependency and addiction. All of these can then lead to unwanted weight gain. Following are some ways to face the problems squarely:

- Talk with others. Say it outright: "I am worried about my weight. Will you help me do something about it?" Come out of the closet of silent suffering. Own the issue and move on.
- Throw away or donate all the cookbooks that maintain or increase the problem, and find new outlets in life—new interests and hobbies that aren't related to food.
- Find any combination of salads, fruits, nuts, vegetables, grains, breads, meats, fish, dairy, legumes that take off—or add, if needed—pounds to bring you to the healthy and desirable weight for yourself and those you love.
- Remove from the kitchen any foods that don't work for you or go against your value system. Find your own "magic" and make it work for you rather than make you suffer. Make the process fun. It's not necessary to convert or convince anyone but you. An increasing number of couples, house-holds, and families eat separate foods at separate times of the day, and each honors the other. It's important for care-givers to understand their own food needs and wants, and then those of their carees so they can help them find their magic as well.

- Take pride in how you look. New haircut, fresh clothes, and a new look go a long way toward feeling good about oneself.
- Have fun with cleaning out old unused dishes and kitchen gadgets and cookware.
- Once you have done this for yourself, help the caree do so as well.

I remember the wisdom of my children's pediatrician, who told me that if my children wanted to eat only peanut butter sandwiches and apple pie—one of them wanted only that diet for six months—to go ahead and let them. That they enjoyed peanuts, a little fat, bread, apples, and a little sugar would eventually even itself out, and they could move on to other single wishes from time to time. In the end, all would equal out. The same is true with an aging population. If popcorn, cereal, bananas, and strawberries are this week's favorite, so be it. Food as an issue is not as important as all the feelings that involve pleasure, stress relief, and impression management. When food returns to simply being fuel, most eating issues of too little or too much disappear.

Food as an issue is not as important as all the feelings that involve pleasure, stress relief, and impression management. When food returns to simply being fuel, most eating issues of too little or too much disappear.

Have fun with food. My soul mate used to say to the grandchildren, "Do not play with your food." It's not all that important whether food is seen as fuel or a plaything. What is important is to get healthy fuel into your body and then move on to more pleasurable activities. Consider how you and your caree eat as your ticket to possibility or limitation.

Sweets   Fast Foods

VS

Fresh Vegetables, Grains, and Fruit

Sharing Food Is Sharing Love

"If you can't feed a hundred people, then feed just one."
—*Mother Teresa*

The old saying that many hands make light work is true when it comes to making sure both caree and caregiver get the regular, healthy meals they both need. It's a daily task that can weigh heavily when one person has to carry the load alone. Preparing and sharing food is another way of saying you care. Providing meals for those who are homebound plays a key role in supporting them and their family. Many ways exist to make sure the caree gets what he or she needs, including the following:

- Meals on Wheels
- using the care visit to bring the caree takeout food
- ordering grocery delivery

Following are a couple of examples of getting help for healthy eating.

Janet. Janet is seventy-four, lives alone, and often forgets to eat. To help her remember, she makes a list of all her favorite foods. Once a week a volunteer takes her to the grocery store. She comes home and posts her list on the refrigerator. She gets out her favorite book, makes one of her favorite meals, and considers every dinner her "special treat time."

Ken. Ken, close to fifty, orders Meals on Wheels for his aging parents. They might not get all they need in between, but he keeps their apartment stocked once a week with fruit, cereal, and canned or packaged soups. He believes that's what he can manage. And the smile he gives them on his weekly stopover is part of the magic that is keeping his parents happy and healthy. Once a month or so, his wife makes something special, such as a cake, pie, or brownies, and his parents feel loved. One of my caregivers told me that she believes "It is not the big things that are important, but rather the small things."

Making the Most of Mealtimes for the Caree

> "Laughter is brightest in the place where food is."
> —*Irish Proverb*

Meals do more than nourish the body. You can make meals the time for connecting and bringing happiness to all involved. A little extra planning and preparation can change a necessity into a memorable moment. Choose food with a meaning or purpose to feed the caree's soul. Special treats and certain meals are memory triggers. Enjoy any special moment you can. For my caree it's meatloaf and mashed potatoes, big bologna sandwiches with fresh tomatoes and lettuce and pudding while watching TV. It all means a lot. So do molasses cookies and ice cream.

Caregivers Caring for Themselves

Making something besides food a reward for themselves is one way caregivers can practice self-care. Caregivers can:

- make a week's worth of healthy food on a day off and bring their own lunches on their route of home visits;
- go out one evening for dinner and bring half of it home for the next night; and
- sign up with a service to have healthy food delivered after a hard day. Even with the abundance of food in our culture, the effort of preparing it after a full day is sometimes just too taxing. Do your best to avoid stress eating at the last minute.

Caregivers can practice saying "no more" to:

- TV eating as a habit can foster loneliness as well as mindless eating. Sometimes the TV is good company. No hard and fast rules here;
- counter eating, which usually means eating mindlessly or too fast, and can be bad for people with heartburn or other digestive issues; and
- last-minute takeout, which is perfect when it's healthy food.

Too often, takeout is processed food, full of salt and fat. It satisfies cravings but leads to extra calories. These are dangerous for our general population, but even more so for people as they age. Choose places that offer fresh food, less salt and fat, and more fruits and vegetables. For those who can afford it or need to do long-distance caregiving, there are companies that will deliver healthy, ready-made meals. Making the effort to find them is worth the time spent.

Another way to self-care with food is to enjoy what you eat. I love to return to childhood comfort meals and re-create them. When I can find recipes, I do, and when I can't find them, I make them up. Many a meal triggers all kinds of memories. Regardless of what food I eat, I also find it important to:

- have fresh flowers or a candle on the table;
- use favorite dishes;
- pretend someone important is coming to dine; someone is—it's me; and
- relax with music, quiet, and reflection.

Whether it's breakfast, lunch, or dinner, plan the hours following eating. Try to find more things than your default activities like TV, laundry, sleep, computer, paying bills, or surfing the Internet. Use food and meals to trigger some joy-filled activity, including the following:

- reading a good book;
- gardening, even if it's only herbs in a container;
- doing a project, such as writing, organizing photos,

creating your family tree, calling a friend, doing some form of art, or playing board games.

Everyone has the same gift of twenty-four hours a day. Choose wisely.

WATER: STAY HYDRATED

"Thousands have lived without love, not one without water."
—W. H. Auden

Like most people, carees and caregivers run the risk of not drinking enough water. To prevent dehydration, we all need to drink adequate amounts of water daily. I recently attended a support group for a friend where a lady there carried a gallon jug of water with her. I live in Colorado, and it's dry here, so we need a great deal of water, and she was making sure she had it. "By nighttime," she told me, "it had better be gone. I have had to teach myself to drink water." She had developed a great tool. Following are a few suggestions to ensure adequate hydration:

- Carry around between a half-gallon to a gallon of water and measure how much you drink.
- Drink different kinds of water to discover a couple that are your go-to waters.
- Drink liquids you love that contain water, such as coffee or tea.
- Savor and appreciate different coffees as well as hot and iced teas.
- Experiment with the volume of water in soups, special drinks, and cereals.
- Fill up your stomach with water before eating; it's easier

to eat much less and can support healthier eating for overeaters.

- Buy a briefcase or bag with a water holder so you are never without it.
- Invest in fun aluminum bottles, and trade comments on collections of water bottles. Eventually have one for each day of the week. Make drinking a fun project.
- Use "ways of drinking water" as a contest between caregiver and caree; have fun with the idea.
- Eat more water. Another way to support hydration is to "eat" your water. Eating fruits and vegetables can help you sidestep drinking too much water, which just ends up getting flushed from your system. The water you take in from eating fruits and vegetables, however, stays longer in your body. Foods with high water content include watermelon, strawberries, cantaloupe, pineapple, oranges, apples, raspberries, iceberg lettuce, celery, broccoli, green peppers, and spinach.
- Carees should avoid drinking water close to bedtime because it might cause too many nighttime trips to the bathroom.

Benefits of Staying Hydrated

- improves the thinking process
- helps you feel refreshed
- supports skin and organ health
- prevents constipation and maintains regularity
- boosts your immune system

- prevents/lessens headaches and muscle cramps
- provides energy
- supports weight management
- clears up bad breath

SHELTER: PEACE AND PRIVACY

"Inside each of us are memories, fantasies and desires for home—
a shelter waiting to be built, a place of peace to be revisited."
—*Louisa Thompsen Brits*

Each caregiver needs to be able to come home to a place of comfort and beauty and replenishment. Find some space that is "just yours" to claim each day. Whether it's a corner or a room, make it yours.

Whether caree or caregiver, home and surroundings need our attention and focus. Each caregiver needs to be able to come home to a place of comfort and beauty and replenishment. Find some space that is "just yours" to claim each day. Whether it's a corner or a room, make it yours. In Chapter 10, we'll look in depth at downsizing and rightsizing as your space needs change over time. If you need to repaint, change furniture, or buy a special chair, give yourself that space and use it each day. If you share space with someone else, claim your privacy.

- If you live alone, build your peaceful sanctuary where you can "fill up" with books, candles, meditation, and comfort foods.

Keep only the essentials, the beautiful, and the useful. Declutter regularly.

- Keep only the essentials, the beautiful, and the useful. Declutter regularly.

- Keep three plastic bins in a closet or corner. One could say Keep, another Donate, and the third Sell. Using these regularly, you will never become overwhelmed with clutter, held down by stuff, and burdened with needing to organize.

Space for the Caree

It is very important for a caree going through changes in their personal lives to have private space. It may be as big as a room of their own, or as small as a table with their hobbies or their books in that spot along with a favorite chair. It is hard for a caree to carve out their "own" space and feel able to make decisions and be independent. This is true also for caregivers. The care is often so enmeshed and immediate that "space" is overlooked, and both parties crave some time away from each other.

Do whatever you can to find some space that is just yours, and go there for a bit each day. When I was a caree and had to remain in my bed for physical reasons, my space was having people understand that I needed to shut the door—just to give me space. For the caregiver, it sometimes means a bath or shower with the door closed, or it can mean watching a TV show alone or taking a walk. Those are small but important gestures to note. Where possible, take bigger spaces and more time alone.

SLEEP: REST EASY

"There is a time for many words and there
is also a time for sleep."
—Homer, "The Odyssey"

Finding time for and getting enough sleep is challenging for many people. Good sleep habits are some of the most important habits we can develop. Proper sleep restores and rejuvenates us, enabling us to grow muscle, repair tissue, and synthesize hormones. In testing, well-rested people are more able to retain information and perform better on memory tasks. There can be many reasons for not getting enough sleep. Here are some ways to improve sleep quality and quantity:

- Power down. Make sure the glow from backups, scanners, cell phones, printers, and digital clocks are covered. Turn off devices if you can. I keep washcloths that match my bedroom décor and cover everything before trying to sleep.
- Try not to nap. Push through the earlier tiredness and plan on a full, longer night of sleep.
- Use a leg pillow to deal with restless leg and find maximum comfort.
- Make sure the mattress fits you as well as your clothes do.
- Have the right number of pillows—and level of firmness—for you.
- Do not work on your bed. Use it only for sleep and sex.
- Watching TV in bed is a personal choice. It helps some people fall asleep, but others experience a negative impact on the quality of their sleep.
- Adjust your sleep habits until you align with your own body clock.
- Try to establish a schedule and stick to it. Go to bed around the same time each night and get up around the same time in the morning; it sets your body's inner clock. Moving

bedtime and waking times can lead to serious inner clock problems.

- Try not to sleep in or catch up on lost sleep. That only invites body-clock problems. Try to treat weekends the same as weekdays.
- Manage sugar and starch intake. They can interfere with sleep cycles and cause daytime sleepiness.
- Determine what level of light in the bedroom works for you. Some may need sleep masks or blackout shades to block light coming through the window at night from streetlights, or moonlight. Others may want to let in morning sun to wake them up. I live in Colorado and get early sun about 300 days a year. So I leave an open strip at the bottom of my blackout shades so I get early light to wake me up.
- Use whatever other sleep devices work for you: earplugs, white noise machines, humidifiers, or fans.
- Spend enough time outside during the day to bring about sleepiness at the regular bedtime.
- Eliminate or cut down on evening screen time on your computer, TV, or cell phone.
- If you experience anxiety as either a caregiver or a caree, start some regular relaxation techniques.
- Be wise about the use of alcohol, which can bring temporary sleepiness followed by wakefulness and an inability to get back to sleep.
- Perhaps the biggest guarantee of regular good sleep habits is exercise, exercise, and more exercise. Find your favorite exercise routine and stick to it regularly.

- Set the scene. Keeping the room between sixty and sixty-five degrees promotes better sleep. Artificial light is also a deterrent to good sleep, while natural early morning sunlight is beneficial.

It is easy to underestimate the importance of sleep as one of our basic five needs in order to survive.

AIR: BREATHE EASY

"I wake up every day and I think, I'm breathing! It's a good day."
—*Eve Ensler*

Breathing not only keeps us alive but also enables us to live to the fullest by using techniques that bring about relaxation and calmness. Let's start with a few facts about the air we breathe.

1. Each time you take a breath, you inhale more than oxygen. Each breath includes three other main gases (nitrogen, argon, and carbon dioxide, plus trace amounts of other gases and water vapor). Different climates and seasons account for the differences in the air we breathe. Study climates, your own need for what kind of air you breathe, and make the best choices you can for you and your caree.

2. Many people have restricted breathing ability due to asthma, chronic obstructive pulmonary disease (COPD), and allergies, etc. It's good to know what is helpful for you or your caree. Either of you might have greater or lesser ease in breathing depending on where you live: in the desert or mountains, by the sea, or in a city. Know which location is best for supporting your health and that of your caree.

3. Use a breathing machine—CPAP—to ensure proper air intake for you or your caree while sleeping. The CPAP provides continuous positive airflow for people who have trouble with sleep apnea, lung issues, or any sleep obstruction. Often a CPAP is used to help stop snoring and ensure that both snorer and partner sleep soundly.

4. Use the 4–7–8 routine or teach your caree how to do it. Exhale completely through your mouth, making a *whoosh* sound. Close your mouth and take a long slow breath through your nose, first filling your lower lungs and then your upper lungs. Inhale to a mental count of four. Hold your breath for a count of seven. Exhale completely through your mouth, making a *whoosh* sound to a count of eight. This is one breath. Now inhale again and repeat the cycle three more times for a total of four breaths.

5. You can also manage stress by relaxing your jaws, shoulders, and face. Be aware that when you get really good at it, you can feel so relaxed that you quickly fall asleep.

6. Investigate breathwork. If you have excessive tension or stress, you will want to investigate the possibility of doing professional breathwork. It's an umbrella term for various breathing practices, which include holotropic rebirthing and Reichian breathing. In breathwork, the conscious control of breathing influences a person's mental, emotional, and/or physical state, with different effects for each person.

7. Different types of yoga techniques can also slow breathing, allow tension relief, and lower anxiety.

RUNNING BEFORE WALKING: A LESSON
FROM BARBARA AND FORMER PRESIDENT BUSH

We all know the excitement of a person who runs around to every kind of spiritual experience, claiming that each is the best they have ever had. Busyness becomes habitual. That same person often struggles with weight, lack of sleep, and eats many of the wrong foods. A few years ago, that syndrome was part of my routine.

At the height of my career, I was facilitating a women's workshop in Texas. The guests had come from all over the United States to hear me speak. I was staying on the fourth floor of a building that was surrounded by artificial turf, about a mile around. I was looking out the window one day when I saw the guests in my workshop go out and run around the building two or three times a day. Then I saw the then president, George H. W. Bush, running around the building (with Secret Service trailing him). And, lo and behold, I saw the First Lady, Barbara Bush, running around the building. She was older than I was. Not to be left out, I went out to do the same. About a third of the way around, I was out of breath. I could hardly walk as I slowly returned to the building. My lack of fitness came as quite a shock.

After the workshop, I called four friends, and we decided to go to Utah to a fitness center. Then called the National Institute of Fitness (NIF), it's now a spa. This started a lifelong love of fitness walking, which I am still doing decades later. The center made walking so much fun. Staying in a geodesic dome, we spent five days of eating vegan, walking until we could walk easily uphill, and resetting every system in my head and body. I graduated from NIF when I could walk five miles uphill. At my graduation, I received a magnetized red STOP sign, which I put on my refrigerator. It remained there until the magnetic charge wore off and wouldn't stick anymore. It didn't mean stop eating. It meant "Stop, think, and choose."

What made these trips different from anything I had ever done before was that I was inspired to change my lifestyle. Soon I was making the time to walk three miles a day. Living in the desert meant very early walking and night-time walking. It also introduced me to walking tapes when I couldn't get outside during the cool hours. Instead of recipe books, I started collecting walking music and couldn't wait to get outside to walk.

I chose to add more foods to the vegan eating plan I had learned at the center, and today I eat anything I want and metabolize everything. Nothing impacts me negatively unless I eat too much sugar or white flour, yet I can eat anything. The guidance I learned at NIF has stayed with me today, and I act on my hard-won knowledge that "nothing tastes as good as feeling healthy feels."

"Nothing tastes as good as feeling healthy feels."

SECTION 2: CAREGIVER AND CAREE ONGOING NEEDS

CONNECTION

"If you want to know who your tribe is, speak your truth.
Then see who sticks around. Those are the people
who get a spot in your blanket fort."
—*Nanea Hoffman*

Do your connections—your family and friends—feed you or drain you? It's very liberating, and at first daunting, to face up to the drain that some family and friends exert on you. It's healthy to evaluate how you spend your time and who and what are contributing to your healthy lifestyle and who and what are taking away from it.

Contributing to healthy or unhealthy connections is a matter of gut feeling. If you find yourself feeling even a tad of anxiety when a certain friend comes to mind, pay attention to it. If any of the following are present in a friend, it's not the best connection for you. Beware the friend who:

- makes you feel guilty that you "should" be doing something different with your time, energy, money, or opinions;
- makes you feel like life is passing you by. He or she is always posting something on social media that makes you wish your life was more like his or hers. Be careful about social media; various posts can regularly make you feel this way. Very few contacts post their broken relationships, their health issues, and their pain. Good for those who do, as social media can also provide great bonding and support. Choose wisely;
- does not give as you give. If you treat, choose family and friends who treat back. If you entertain people at home, choose friends who entertain in return;
- becomes a downer every time you talk, a Chicken Little for whom the sky is always falling. The sky can be overcast, but it's not falling down. Choose friends who make your soul sing;
- takes up precious time with every contact without considering your time and energy.

Often caregivers are amazed when they keep a time log and see how many important hours are wasted on connection in relationships that drain their energy. It often happens on the phone or computer, less so in person. When we meet face-to-face with someone, it's

Often caregivers are amazed when they keep a time log and see how many important hours are wasted on connection in relationships that drain their energy.

easier to measure each person's involvement. Phones and computers can be deceiving. It's time to weigh our lifestyles.

CONNECTION

"Cherish your human connections,
your relationships with friends and family."
—Joseph Brodsky

As José N. Harris tells us: "There comes a time in your life, when you walk away from all the drama and people who create it. You surround yourself with people who make you laugh. Forget the bad, and focus on the good. Love the people who treat you right, pray for the ones who don't. Life is too short to be anything but happy. Falling down is a part of life; getting back up is living."

As José N. Harris tells us: "There comes a time in your life, when you walk away from all the drama and people who create it. You surround yourself with people who make you laugh. Forget the bad, and focus on the good. Love the people who treat you right, pray for the ones who don't. Life is too short to be anything but happy. Falling down is a part of life; getting back up is living."

In one of my earlier books, *Choicemaking*, the subtitle indicated that it was for codependents, adult children, and spirituality seekers. If I were writing it today, I would add that it is also for caregivers. As we go forward in choosing self-care, we might need to change friendships and relationships. This has always been a tough one for me.

When my children were in grade school and high school, I was also attending college, getting my education. It left me with little or no time to nourish friendships. At one point, I remember going to all my close friends—one by one—and speaking my truth. I let them each know what they meant to me.

Preparing to do that was a good exercise in gratitude and awareness. Some actually meant a great deal more to me than did others. My friends fell into two groups: nourishing and not as nourishing. I told them, in the most honest way I could, that I needed time, focus, and energy. I told them that between my marriage, my children, and my education, I was cutting out lunches, camping trips, long coffees, and opinion fests. This was in the 1960s, and long talks after class were a part of life in the afternoon.

I also let go of long dinner parties and lengthy phone calls. What I needed to do for me was study, spend time with my kids, eat healthy, exercise, and get regular sleep. I also told my friends that I would be ready to reevaluate in about two years when I graduated. Then I set about for a lifestyle change. It was really not that hard to do once I had focused and made up my mind.

Interestingly, only a very few people were offended and shocked at this idea. Most supported me and are part of my inner circle to this day. I really didn't miss the rest, and I never needed to reevaluate. I have changed my lifestyle many times, added friends, and stopped wasting time on friendships that drain me. So choose carefully. Let go and keep the best.

I like to refer to that inner circle as the people in my blanket fort. Most children make blanket forts by spreading blankets or sheets over chairs and tables and play underneath with their friends. My blanket fort is almost a sacred space. It's where I feel comfortable sharing secrets with my friends and many family members. It's a very full and nourishing space.

P.S. Many of my friends have built blanket forts as well.

First Things First: Reconnect with—and Invest in—Yourself

"There's only one corner of the universe you can be certain
of improving, and that's your own self."
—*Aldous Huxley*

It's really a thrill to have new adventures and live a pattern
of travel, seeking, and exploring. It's a way of reconnecting with
yourself and life. Being the "best you" is the ideal way to add to
your life. To ease the stress and relentlessness of being a caregiver,
formal and informal, do it in a healthy way.

Perhaps take the time and make the commitment to get yourself
in the best personal condition and then set about to develop your
lifestyle around those choices. Instead of saying, "I don't have time,"
say, "I will make time." Instead of saying, "I'll grab something
quick," say, "I'm going to choose something healthy for me." Instead
of saying, "I will make good choices after the holiday, when the
weather gets better, or when I feel better, or when I get caught up"
... make the choices now.

This is the time. As Hillel, an ancient Jewish sage and scholar,
said: "If I am not for myself, who is for me?" He later added, "If
not now, when?" You won't be able to do everything at once, but
decide that now is the time to invest in yourself and get started with
a plan. Give that gift to yourself and then add to your plan from
there. There will always be conferences, a place in the world you
haven't seen, and people to be with. There will never be another
you. Make the investment in your "self" and

*There will never be
another you.*

then make choices that bring you happiness,
contentment, connection, relationships, and
health.

TRANSPORTATION IN CAREGIVING

*"Transportation is the center of our world.
It is the glue of our daily lives. When it goes well, we don't see it.
When it goes wrong, it negatively colors our day,
makes us feel angry, and impotent,
curtails our possibilities."*
—*Robin Chase*

Filling your toolbox with as much information as possible on transportation needs and solutions is an important part of caregiving. Of course, such options exist as family members donate their time, and many informal, unpaid caregivers can handle the transportation needs of the caree. A whole array of transportation options for caregivers has arrived with Uber, Lyft, and Via to complement traditional transport by bus, taxi, train, friends, volunteer agencies, and paid caregivers.

Do your research and fill your toolbox with as many options as are available and cost-effective where you live. For example, in my home we use Lyft, Uber, a volunteer agency, and a paid caregiver.

A sixty-year-old I know was in pain recently and called 911 asking if he should go to the hospital. Since it didn't sound like an emergency, they advised that he see his primary care doctor. The man lives alone and is doing his best to age in place. He tried two of his friends who were not home. His pain was very difficult for him. He then called Uber, which his daughter had put on his phone. Uber delivered him to an urgent care center where they discovered a serious situation requiring surgery. He was told that if he had not come in, there would have been grave consequences.

Getting the right information and making tough decisions to make a manageable and comfortable lifestyle is something we can all do. Eliminating gaps in the transportation chain is a big part of coordinating care for a caree. A solid transportation plan can free up time and reduce stress and caregiver fatigue.

As caregivers experience overwhelm with day-to-day care, there is a growing awareness that more funding and resources are needed. While they cannot be out raising money for the problem at large and take care of their carees' daily needs, they can stay abreast of what is going on in the world. They can find out who publically represents the community of care and vote accordingly. It is important for caregivers to use their voice to help the development of further resources.

SAFETY

Caregivers cannot be "on alert" at all times for their carees. A great number of alert devices are available that don't force the caregiver to live in a constant state of hypervigilance. Get informed and fill your toolbox with any technology or technique that reduces anxiety about your caree's safety. A few of the better-known devices are Life Alert, ADT, MobileHelp, LifeStation, and Medical Guardian. You can find information on these and others online.

Getting a family member to use a medical alert system, a cane, a wheelchair, a walker, or hearing aid is a big step. To accomplish this may fall in the range of tough love and tough decision making. Do your best and then love yourself for it. Part of tough love is the caregiver loving himself or herself enough to cope with and handle caree resistance. Always remember, you did your best and then go on. Strong resiliency is a gift you give yourself.

RESILIENCE

Resiliency is the capacity to recover quickly from difficulties. It is a certain kind of toughness. Some of the most important teachers in my life showed me resiliency. One was a fragile-looking aunt who was always available when I needed help as a child and then as an adult. She probably weighed 110 pounds, was never afraid of catching a cold or flu from someone else, and lived through stress and trauma some can only imagine. Her resiliency was a great teacher for me.

Another model for me was a man who cried at every parade and wedding and funeral. His ability to feel his emotions deeply and often was the most masculine and attractive display of resiliency. Another was a man who took care of his mother, who in her dementia was extremely unkind to him. She went so far as to insult him, accused him of being selfish, and once threw a book at him. He set boundaries with her: no physical abuse was permitted. Then went about his own life with grace and quiet authority. That was a great example of resiliency.

One more is a woman I know who is as beautiful inside as she is outside. She lost two children to suicide. Yet she continues to provide a nurturing home to her husband and remaining two children. She volunteers in a suicide prevention clinic and is active in her life with good friends and works part time.

Resiliency lives within each caregiver and can be nourished and built upon with each event. Go for it!

SECTION 3: CAREGIVER AND CAREE THRIVING NEEDS

Interestingly, once the basic and ongoing needs for each are secure, both caregivers and carees share the same needs to thrive and be fulfilled on this journey together.

PURPOSE

Three things all people need in order to prosper and find inner peace and contentment is some "one" to love, some "one" to be loved by, and some "thing" to do. You get some of all those in simply "being" a caregiver. Celebrate yourself. You have a whole life, and being a caregiver is not your entire role. You are fulfilling a life purpose every time you do a caregiver act. Blessings to you. Give yourself credit and a pat on the back each time you act. You have made a great contribution to this life.

Three things all people need in order to prosper and find inner peace and contentment is some "one" to love, some "one" to be loved by, and some "thing" to do.

The caree's primary purpose is to get better to the fullest extent he or she can, while allowing oneself to be taken care of. That's not always easy in a society that values independence and self-reliance, but it's vital to thrive as a caree.

A caree feels deeply about and battles with no longer being independent. One has to work hard to accept, surrender, and know that "just being" is important to the people who love you. One has to challenge love relationships, and daily—sometimes hourly—repeat this mantra to oneself: "My existing purpose is to help provide purpose to another." If the caree cannot feel that mantra, then perhaps he or she also does not feel the need to be independent or self-reliant. Both the caree and the caregiver have to trust that what is felt by the caree is what is possible and needed at that time.

It also takes energy, determination, knowledge, and love to recover. That is a simple truth. Both the caree and the caregiver have a big job to feel, accept feelings, accept thoughts, and find actions that work for both of them. Love is both known and felt.

SELF-RESPECT

Caring for one who has many needs, ever present and ongoing, is demanding. One must develop a sense of self-knowing and consider caring for self as important as caring for others. Each toolbox needs to have a defined list of what it takes to care for oneself. It may differ from one person to another: Some need alone time, others need social time. Some need to nap, others need space.

My family is an example. When the family gathered on a holiday or celebrations, one member would often disappear for a while. Conversations continued, sometimes heated, other times entertaining, and often quite involved. Suddenly we would notice that someone was missing. It usually meant he was in his room—reading an article or taking a "quick nap." When questioned about his disappearance, he simply said, "When there is a great deal happening at once, I tune out. I know I need a break, so I take it." He respected himself to know when he needed a time-out.

For the caree, the event or illness that initiated the need for care may have involved a loss of position or function. Going from having authority and responsibility to being dependent may cause a loss of self-respect. The caree is not the person he or she was. But he or she still needs to remember their worth as a person—someone worthy of attention and love.

RELIEF

Relief and self-respect are similar, but relief is a longer break from duty and stress. In my case, my sister needed to share a serious diagnosis with me and to tell me all the details so she and I could be close as she struggled with her health. To me, some details were very serious, others less so. To her, they were all serious. Sometimes, however, I was so full of her struggle that I couldn't feel or respond to my own needs at that time. Occasionally, I had to back away for days when I could not listen to more or respond. It became clear to me that on weekdays, I could be there for her, but on weekends, I could not. I needed to replenish and remember my own identity, so I did not take her phone calls from Friday to Monday, which gave me great relief. Monday to Thursday, I listened with love and care.

One way for the caree to find relief is by detaching from their condition. It's not always easy. But it's easier when we remember that we are not our illnesses. We have life stories and relationships, we have accomplishments and contributions. And above all, we have connections that remind us that we are valued. But in cases where mental capacity has markedly declined—or a diagnosis is terminal—relief may be impossible.

TIME

An important concept to me is "timeless time." This concept comes up in almost all my writings. It's the time I don't have to account for, and everyone needs a certain amount of it. My rhythm is taking an hour a day, a half day a week, a weekend a month, and two weeks a year. No calls or visits with explanations required. It's my self-nourishment. Circumstances are different for everyone. The important thing is to decide what time you need for you and when.

A caree might also need time out. A time when he or she is free from visits, questions, and interruptions. This is also one of the times in life when a little bit of denial is acceptable. Some days both the caree and caregiver would just like to have a fantasy day to "pretend" that everything is okay again.

SAVORING

Someone taught me this lesson a long time ago. We all have had good things and bad things in our lives. I have often spoken of the bad, good, better, and best. When things are bad, we all want something good. Once we get what is good, it's natural to want more—better. Once we get something more, and when we have more things, we want the best. Once we have the best, then the time comes when our life is "so full of the best things," we don't take the time to enjoy them. This is where savoring comes in.

Whether it's a meal, a visit, a phone call, a beautiful day of gorgeous weather, stop, take it in, and savor it. It will mean many choices. You might have to give up "one of the best things in your life" in order to have the time to enjoy other best things.

You might have to give up "one of the best things in your life" in order to have the time to enjoy other best things.

The capacity to savor may seem out of reach when you're ill, in pain, and afraid. But that's when it may be most important. When you regain a function you've lost, take pleasure in it. Regaining what has been lost is deeply satisfying. Simple things like sitting up, walking, eating on your own, or reading and writing can bring a great deal of happiness. And it's good to know that there is always more to regain.

TOOLS FOR HANDLING HOTSPOTS

"Relationships cannot grow without the proper form of communication."
—*Anonymous*

We have covered the basic needs and their accompanying tools. But it's also important to be aware of a few common pitfalls when conflict arises. Being alert to time, to act, topics to avoid, and potentially diminished capacities can make life while caregiving—and care receiving—that much easier. Following are five tools that can help you avoid or reduce hotspots:

1. TIMING

When you or your caree is in pain or tired, it is not the best time to talk about important issues. Caregivers become frustrated when they too often have to make many decisions and feel the stress of being both the decision maker and the action planner. Carees feel resentful that they are losing independence when they don't get to make those decisions themselves. It becomes increasingly important that the caree and the caregiver discuss what needs to be resolved. Choose a time when both parties are able to fully engage to hear each other and make necessary agreements. Some people are morning people, others are more alert in the afternoon, or still others are early evening people.

Tool: find your best time and use it.

2. RED FLAG SUBJECTS

All carees and caregivers have red flag subjects. Divorce, death, money, politics, and religion are common subjects. Aunt Mabel's inheritance, Mom's way of shopping, and Dad's complaints about handling the car might top one's list. And the list goes on and on. Many subjects are best left alone in caregiving times. Pick your discussions and disagreements. Save the decision making and strong feelings for the subjects that matter. What was fodder for lively discussions and long conversations in more stress-free times is now a luxury most families and jobs cannot afford at this time of life.

Tool: choose a fun activity over discussion of tender topics. Share a nice meal, play cards or a board game. Or talk about a movie or TV show.

3. OLD FEELINGS AND HURTS

Some hurts and slights will never be healed. "Mom loved you best" is now old news, yet the hurt lingers. Anger, competition, and old wounds can rear their ugly heads when new subjects come up.

Tool: if a caree and caregiver are willing, bring the family together and give each member of the group a chance to write down one or two long-term hurts that still rankle. Then to symbolize letting go of the hurts, gather the slips of paper and bury them in a flowerpot with lots of dirt, or, if weather permits, bury them outside. Then ask the group if they are willing to bury old hurts and make the next months and years the best yet.

4. JUDGING ONESELF ON RANK

You have a very important role when much of your job is connected to the well-being of another human being. In many branches of caregiving there is a perceived rank order. What the specialist says is sometimes seen as more important than the opinion of the primary caregiver, which ranks higher than an assistant's input, and so on down the line regarding the registered nurse, the licensed practical nurse, the technician, and all the way to the aide. Most rankings reflect standards for determining pay and even benefits.

However, in terms of what the caree finally receives, rank is unimportant. Each rank involves the care of a human being. Every position is equally important and should be viewed as such. Some of my best rehabilitation came from the housekeeper and the meal coordinator.

Tool: if you are involved in any level of care for any other human being, give yourself a pat on the back and appreciate your contribution.

5. HOW MUCH TO SHARE WITH OTHERS

With aging memory loss, dementia of any kind, Alzheimer's disease, or any other diminished thought processes, arguments and bickering often derail conversations. Any two people—caree or caregiver—will see things differently. If they are strong personalities, many arguments will occur. It's wise to involve a third person when the arguing or bickering starts coloring conversations.

When it's apparent that a diminished thinking process is interfering with communication, it may be prudent to share less with the caree to avoid conflict. This is a slippery slope, as less communication might mean less agreement, information sharing, and intimacy. But weighed carefully, wisdom and discernment is necessary.

Tool: do some third-party checking with your support system.

MORE TOOLS FOR MAKING THE MOST OF EACH DAY

"You never lose by loving. You always lose by holding back."
—Barbara De Angelis

Caregiving is hard work. But there is no reason not to plan for and be alert to every opportunity for fun. You can plan for fun times in ways big and small.

- **Plan events.** They may be new and different kinds of events with each new normal. Half the fun is the anticipation.
- **Reframe the ordinary.** Adding popcorn and a favorite drink transforms watching a TV show to going to the movies.
- **Other simple ideas.** Try one or more of these activities that can make a big difference in your day: read to the caree; choose TV programs of mutual interest and joy; read the same book and set aside a time each day to discuss a paragraph or two; listen to music together; just hold hands, which brings warmth and connection; share old photos; and share memories of holidays, trips, and events.
- **Say thank you.** Spend a little time each day thinking about the gratitude both caregiver and caree have for each other. This attitude goes a long way. Keeping a gratitude list and referring to it regularly each week is a reliable mood lifter.

- **Create a "respect" list.** It's amazing how far cooperation in caregiving goes once the focus is on what went right instead of anything that went wrong. Caregiver, tell the caree all the things that helped. Caree, say thank you and give a smile to your caregiver.
- **Forget "I forgot."** Use Post-it Notes on a counter or refrigerator to identify each task that needs to be done. As each item is completed, throw away that note. These reminders make everyone on the care team feel "counted in the action."
- **Celebrate each occasion.** Birthdays, holidays, and anniversaries—and the times in between—are filled with anticipation and memories. There are so many things to celebrate year-round. I have set up a Holiday Corner, where I remember each special celebration and culture until the next one comes along.

    Christmas, Hanukkah, and Festival of Lights and New Year's (Western and Chinese)

    St. Patrick's Day, Easter, Cinco de Mayo, Mother's Day, and Memorial Day

    Father's Day, Fourth of July, Labor Day, and Halloween

- **Practice the magic of "So?"** A good friend listens to me when I have a complaint, a worry, or feel overwhelmed. When I finish and take a breath, she says "So?" and then I go into more of my issue. When I'm done, she says, "So?" again, and I go on until I have worked through my issue. She is a great therapist and all she has said is "So?" and I feel much better. She has taught me to do this on my own, but sometimes it's really good to work through it with a friend.

- **Play board and card games.** The distraction of a game and the time spent with a friend lessens the day's stress. Playing games is something caregivers can do for themselves and carees can do with each other that can strengthen the bond between them. Some games pass through agencies, down families, and become bonding tools. Playing cards are especially portable—and inexpensive. Many individuals and families remember some special connection times around the games of hearts, cribbage, bridge, canasta, poker, and many more. It is a great tool and a form of therapy for many families.

- **Have a master calendar in your open area.** When more than one person is involved in your life, it helps to have a master calendar. Record medical appointments, family reminders, caregivers, events, birthdays, etc., all in one place. It brings order to one's day-to-day living.

A FINAL TOOL: SHOW UP AND LISTEN

"The quieter you become, the more you can hear."
—Ram Dass

My good friend Ted shared his concept of "showing up" with me. Sometimes it's all we can do, but it's also one of the most important. Of course, it's what is needed most. Showing up is evident in holding hands, the smiles, the touch, the eye contact, and the words of hope and comfort. Healing happens in those ways. Ted has shown up in my home over the years for many reasons. He has contributed to my healing process in "showing up."

Another way to show up is to send cards, flowers, and e-mail letters. Phone calls can be appropriate but also inconvenient for a number of reasons: bad timing when doctors and nurses are in the room, difficult sleeping hours, different time zones, and many more. When I was recovering from a fall, it took months of recovery. One friend sent a card almost every ten days for many of those months. That was a beautiful way to show up.

Listening is another way to show up. In our hustle and bustle lifestyle, to feel heard is healing and a gift. Caregivers and companion carers know the importance of listening.

> "All we have to decide is what to do with
> the time that is given us."
> —*J. R. R. Tolkien*

TECHNOLOGY AND CAREGIVING

*The advance of technology is based on
making it fit in so that you don't really even
notice it, so it's part of everyday life*

—Bill Gates

The impact of technology on caregiving is so strong that it merits its own chapter as a tool. Technology enables caregivers and carees to do more and much more easily: to connect, to manage more effectively, to be more independent, and to save time and effort in everyday functions.

Perhaps this whole book was born on a visit my son made to Las Vegas when I lived there. It was in early 2010. As far as I was concerned, I was long retired. I had sold my company, retired to a fifty-five-plus community, and become a tap dancer. I had also retired my portable Smith Corona typewriter. In the late '70s and early '80s, I had handwritten my manuscripts with a lead pencil or I typed them on that Corona.

> *"We are going shopping for an iPad."*
> *"A what?" I said.*
> *So began my journey of technology.*

My son said, "We are going shopping for an iPad."

"A what?" I said. So began my journey of technology.

I took up writing again, and here I am today at my desktop. Technology has been the most liberating, frustrating, helpful, limiting, joy-filled, frustration-filled, and satisfying part of my older years. It's a most necessary part of my life in many ways.

Technology is important for both the caregiver and the caree. Each day, more technology is added to our lives, assigning the caregiver two roles. One is using everything in their work that helps them do the job at hand—making the caree's life better by meeting the physical and emotional needs of the caree by handling issues around food, transportation, medical care, housing, financial assistance, etc.

The second role, increasingly important with a new generation of caregivers, is enabling carees to do more self-care with the addition of learning technology. In addition to traditional caregiver roles, we now have many families who have a tech family person or persons more familiar with the devices, services, and software that can improve carees' lives.

The first step in the process of using technology is learning what is available, helpful, and "doable." A commitment to ongoing learning can seem daunting at first but is the key to fitting technology into your life—and maybe even having a bit of fun in the process.

The focus with technology is often to overcome carees' concerns (or even the caregivers' anxiety themselves) that they just don't get it—and don't want to. Sometimes they say, "I am too old to learn this computer stuff," or "I don't have the patience to work through it." Often, that is because they did not previously have or use technology tools before they became a caree. Trying to learn something new on this level while being a caree can feel overwhelming.

Yet in today's fast-paced, interconnected world, using technology to connect with friends and family—as well as with the larger world—is critical, especially for a caree who wants to age in place. Being able

> *Yet in today's fast-paced, interconnected world, using technology to connect with friends and family—as well as with the larger world—is critical.*

to meet some of your daily needs using the same products and services as your friends and family members gives a sense of satisfaction and accomplishment.

Finding simple and useful ways to apply technology is an important and key challenge. With so much information available, it is necessary to "keep your plan simple" and find manageable ways to use technology. I call that making technology work for you instead of you working for technology.

Most carees don't want to turn over their health records, financial information, and personal data to a professional or paid caregiver. Thus, it's imperative that carees learn to cooperate with a trusted friend/family member who can help with this part of receiving care. They can create a "Care Support Team" who uses technology to coordinate care. Caregiving technology can help you to support your caree and make life easier and more manageable in several of the following ways:

- **Connection:** As an increasing number of us choose to age in place, it is important for us as well as the caree to stay connected with friends, family, and professional contacts.
- **Two-Way Virtual Video Conversation:** Tools like Skype or FaceTime allow the caree to instantly bridge the communication gap, to be virtually present with another person, and can serve as a well-being monitor. Of course, it's just fun staying linked to loved ones. In addition, sharing and exchanging photos is a wonderful way to stay connected and participate in each other's lives.
- **Shopping:** Mobility issues and the lack of walkable neighborhoods often make it necessary for carees to meet their basic needs by shopping remotely. Online shopping is available for groceries, household goods, clothing, medical supplies, and prescriptions. The caree can set up accounts with a credit card so all they have to do is place the order. With new voice-activated services like Alexa or Google Home Assistant, they don't even need a computer or smartphone—they just tell the device to place an order directly. An itemized record of past purchases is also available, which is helpful at tax time.
- **Financial Management:** Monthly bills as well as repeat payments, such as insurance, can be automated, which allows the caree comfort in knowing that they won't "forget" a payment. Many financial institutions (banks, investment firms, and utilities) have apps that make it easy to deposit checks, pay bills, and check balances using a computer or smartphone.
- **Health Services:** An increasing number of doctors,

hospitals, and health care providers are moving to electronic records, which enable better record retention, sharing information quickly, and more accurate data collection. To input and access this critical information, patients are often encouraged to use an online portal. Working with carees to set up and use these resources will streamline the medical management process.

- **Activities:** Many carees are reluctant or unable to go out in evenings to attend cultural/social events as often as they would like. The ability to stream TV, movie, and music content can make a boring day a bit brighter. New smart TVs and streaming devices enable choices like never before—but often come with a blizzard of confusing remote controls, instructions, and passwords. The ability to use even a portion of these services online will enable the caree to feel connected to the world in a way that makes sense for them.

- **Artificial Intelligence:** Although it goes by many names, AI, the growing prevalence of the "Internet of things," means that once private systems, such as cars, appliances, home heating and cooling controls, and security cameras, are increasingly interconnected and online. Someone needs to be responsible to navigate the instructions, set up the devices to work properly, and then to tie them into existing Bluetooth/Wi-Fi networks.

These activities are just a few of the ways that technology plays an ever increasing important role in the life of a caregiver and caree. However, challenges and barriers exist to using many of these devices and services. Some of those include the following:

- The need to set up and recall assorted passwords and logins for multiple devices and services.
- Frequent software updates that must be downloaded and installed to make sure the devices continue to function properly.
- Concerns about privacy and online fraud scare carees from even starting down the technology path.
- Incompatible hardware and software that don't "play well together" is frustrating. Proprietary software makes this more likely.
- Backup issues: Make sure the information you have entrusted to a computer can be restored if it is lost.
- Troubleshooting: who do you call when something doesn't work? The "tech world" has its own language. The acronyms can be baffling (PDF, IOT, SAAS, and so on), and too often it is assumed that the user process, such as swiping a phone screen, is an innate skill. Apps and software add to the mix and offer a plethora of options—which adds to feeling overwhelmed with it all.

My approach to introducing new technology is to start, quite literally, at the beginning and not assume any prior knowledge. This includes getting familiar with the device interface, which can be intimidating to anyone who has not grown up with it. Following are tips I use to get a caree comfortable with a device or service:

- Take a picture of the screen or device to be used and then mark on it each button's function.
- Label cords for charging or connection, so if they are moved, they can be quickly put back in the right place.

- Practice storage and retrieval of key information so that carees know where to find important files.
- Diagram the sequence of steps for each necessary action. For example, how to open and reply to an e-mail message. The key is to have the caree write the instructions in his or her own words, making it more likely to stick and serve as a helpful resource if they get lost in the future.

When helping carees learn to use new technology or a device, I have often had to literally sit on my hands instead of jumping in to "just do it myself." It may be easier for the moment, but you risk creating a dependency that makes the caree feel as if they cannot do it themselves. There is a time to have someone else do the computing, but the more comfortable the carees are with the activities that are important to them, the more empowered they will be, and the more willing they are to try new things.

It is better to be good at a few key activities than to try to master them all. Those will vary by individual, but the ability to connect and engage with technology will make life better for the caregiver and caree. Getting the caree to be an active, eager learner is ideal.

My son taught me valuable lessons about technology:

- I can learn more than I ever thought possible.
- Public libraries are a very good resource for learning some of this technology, as are night schools.
- Teaching needs to be clear, useful, and possible.
- The field of technology is more overwhelming than imagined.
- An entirely new category of technicians/tech instructors are needed to build a bridge between those who know how

to navigate the caregiving technology with those who have limited technological skill. Sometimes a family team member can review a medical report with the caree during a conference call on a smartphone, tablet, or computer.

The ideal would be for each caregiver and each caree to have a tech supporter and teacher to help them keep up with the necessary technology.

The ideal would be for each caregiver and each caree to have a tech supporter and teacher to help them keep up with the necessary technology.

CAREE AND CAREGIVER MAJOR TOOLS

"Technology is nothing. What's important is that you have faith in people, that they're good and smart, and if you give them tools, they'll do wonderful things with them."
—*Steve Jobs*

As a senior, I've embraced technology in bits and pieces, as the need arises. The following is a list of tools I am currently using, and I am sure I will continue to add more in the future. These tools allow me, at age eighty, to work with my caregivers and to be a caregiver at the same time.

- **A desktop computer** connects me to family and friends; allows me to shop on Amazon; teaches me through the Internet; stores all my valuable papers; and connects me to a word processor, printer, and scanner. It lets me write books, listen to music, and Skype, while keeping my passwords safe and storing all my treasured photos.

- **An iPad** allows me to take most computer functions with me wherever I go. It was a lifesaver when I was in the rehabilitation center, for I had the ability to play music, watch TV, catch up on e-mail, and surf the Internet with a device I held in my hand. It was a game changer.

- **E-readers,** such as Kindle, and tablets enable downloading of books for free from the library—and enlarging type for easier reading. Backlit screens also allow seniors to see the text better.

- **A smartphone** keeps me safely connected to my small and big worlds. It also serves as a one-stop shop as a camera, video recorder, microphone, flashlight, speaker, magnifying glass, and many other tools all in one small package.

- **A scanner** is one of my most important devices. It enables me to work with my lawyer, my accountant, my family, and my financial manager. It saves data from paper files, helps me e-mail, and saves me the time and effort of having to leave home to transmit information. It allows me to talk to vendors by showing them scanned photos of objects. It often eliminates that expensive "first call for repair" on a home visit, which saves me money. It also allows me to save important documents to my computer storage instead of having so much paper. I can't imagine, as a senior, not having a scanner.

- **A backup system** is vital. Because I store digital versions of many official documents, I need a reliable backup system so I won't lose everything. I have had to use my backup system twice to recover stored data that was lost on my desktop.

- **Wall clocks,** though not high-tech items, work for me. My family lives in different time zones, so knowing what time it is where they live makes me feel connected to them when I contact them. Four small wall clocks tell me the time in each time zone. It makes life easier.

- **A printer** is very important to me, allowing me to print and store documents. Some things I need to see and touch in order to feel safe. Together with one file cabinet, I am not paperless.

- **My iPod** is an old-fashioned but beloved device. Even though there are many ways to carry music, I still love my iPod. It is old—maybe even valuable by now—but it gives me great energy and activates memories. Not only did it teach me to love walking twenty-five years ago, but also hearing the old songs I have stored on it is comforting and reminds me of the choices I made when I started to exercise. I also appreciate the music of my era.

- **A DVD player** is even older technology but one that keeps me exercising indoors when poor weather prevents outdoor activity. I walk to walking tapes and have a class by myself. Also, I love to catch up on old movies and family movies. Some have been converted to flash drives, so it's even easier to share with friends.

- **A smart TV** is used for entertainment, learning, relaxation, and connecting to the wider world. Movies, documentaries, and classes provide great possibilities. Sometimes, a small TV posed in my bathroom allows me to relax and catch up on my day. It's the salt and pepper to a very active life.

Learning the system of network TV, plus all the streaming possibilities, and knowing just enough about remotes and delivery systems makes it a great tool for me. It has opened doors and added many choices to my life.

- **A car starter** is a must for chilly mornings. I love my car being warm on cold Colorado days. I just hit a couple of buttons in the house, and then I can get into a warm car.

- **A garage door opener** is less of a luxury and more of a necessity. Living in a cold climate makes for some mighty chilly trips to the car. Having a garage door opener is important.

- **A Bose radio** and speakers may be one of my steadiest pleasures. I am in the area for KGUD radio, which plays all my favorite music from 6:00 AM to 6:00 PM. Each of the announcers feels like a friend. Sunday afternoon, all scheduled happenings stop so nothing will interfere with my two hours of rare rock 'n' roll. Snow sometimes interferes with reception, leaving me with a few hours without this station and experiencing withdrawal and loss.

- **Alexa** is another world of its own; one I am exploring. So far, Alexa provides news and sports updates, weather reports, movie previews, music, phone answering, and recipes as part of my daily life. Pods on each floor and in the garage make a phone available to me at all times.

I remember the days when it would have been hard to live without a microwave, dishwasher, or washer/dryer, as I did for most of my childhood. Now it would be unthinkable to live without

I remember the days when it would have been hard to live without a microwave, dishwasher, or washer/dryer, as I did for most of my childhood. Now it would be unthinkable to live without a cell phone, computer, scanner, or printer. Times do change, and we adapt quickly to technological advances.

a cell phone, computer, scanner, or printer. Times do change, and we adapt quickly to technological advances.

THE CAREGIVING FAMILY

Family is not an important thing.
It's everything.

—Michael J. Fox

As we saw in Chapter 2, most caregiving comes from the family. An estimated 44 million or more Americans—mothers, fathers, daughters, sons, brothers, sisters, and other relatives—provide unpaid care to an adult or child family member caree.

Each family will generally face caregiving in much the same way they approach their family system of communication. It can be a difficult experience. A few family systems have unique and specific problems with communication. The painful and emotionally shutdown families usually have a member who is suffering from addiction, which removes him or her from contributing to a healthy family system. This person can be someone with any one or more of the following:

1. An alcohol problem.
2. Nicotine addiction.
3. A drug (prescription or illegal) problem; thus, relating to someone medicated is an issue in its own right.
4. Dependency on one of the process addictions.
   - Work
   - Screens (computer, phone, Internet, or social media)
   - Sex
   - Food and eating
   - Exercise

Each couple, with or without children, find their way of communicating. The families of joy and openness as a system will produce happy, productive, and independent children who will go on to do the same in their families. Families with unresolved pain will produce children of pain who will go on and do the same unless they seek help to change. Sometimes the pain is obvious while other times it is subtle. Books, degrees, certificates, and industries are available to specifically address each of these types of families. Let me briefly take you through just a couple.

BROKEN FAMILY SYSTEM

When families that have not learned how to communicate become caregivers, they lack the ability to connect with one another, and the roles we saw in Chapter 2—Team Captain, Helper, Avoider, and Blamer—become fixed and rigid. They can't connect with one another and work together as a team. This I call the Broken Family caregiving system.

Family members stay busy with work, pleasure, holidays, trips, and anything else that helps avoid honestly facing one another and talking about their feelings and the pain of reality. Avoidance becomes a style of communication.

Each person plays the game, and each person suffers alone inside. This often occurs with families going through a divorce, families who have serious money problems, families dealing with workaholism, and families whose members have been hurt in general.

In a broken family system, there seem to be many unspoken rules. It is simply understood without anyone stating it that avoidance is the general rule of thumb. They do not talk about money, politics, and feelings. Most of the conversation is practical and functional. It is as though emotional, gut-feeling language doesn't exist. Members of a broken family share little that is personal and even less about feelings. Periodically anger blows up, letting off steam, and then communication settles back into pleasantries, function, and information. They share companionship and time together but little intimacy. There is often hysterical laughter but not much humor. Angry outbursts are seldom balanced by direct, constructive anger. Guilt remains private and shame stays unspoken. It is painful to live in a broken system, but many families live out their lives this way.

When a crisis comes—and crises are part of life—the family swings into caregiving in the same way. They tend to choose support and friends who also avoid and create a bubble of avoiding the tough stuff. Issues such as sex, relationships, financial standing, anger, disappointment, and political beliefs are all avoided, and "nice and polite" get played out.

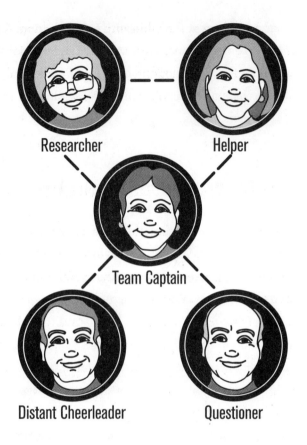

Researcher   Helper

Team Captain

Distant Cheerleader   Questioner

FAMILY FRIENDLY TEAM

Families that have learned to communicate are able to share their feelings, collaborate, and acknowledge and celebrate one another's contributions. This I call the Family Friendly Team.

They are connected. They talk about the reality of what is happening. To these family members, feelings are facts. Feelings "just are," and they may be different for each person involved, yet everyone is heard and feelings are felt, negotiated, and responded to. Everyone has a place at the table with equal sharing. A family friendly team lets go of old hurts, resentments, and opinions and is open to hearing new input, thoughts they don't necessarily agree with, and plans that call for cooperation. They allow no room for blame and judgment.

FAMILY MEMBER ROLES IN CAREGIVING

It is important to understand that the following roles are not fixed but rather possibilities, and no one is in any role all of the time. The roles represent the needs the family has at different times and in different situations; members can switch their roles to provide what is needed. Perhaps one person is the Captain for Mom and a different child is the Captain for Dad. Perhaps no one in the family is taking on the role of Questioner or Researcher, so nothing gets done. Perhaps everyone lives in the same city and they have no long-distance Cheerleaders.

These roles are useful, however, to understand the dynamics in a family system. Once named and understood, a language emerges that makes conversation and behavior easier to understand. In other words, the roles aid communication.

- **Team Captain:** Every family has a team leader, just as a sports team has a captain who holds the group together. This person takes on the role of being dependable and hands-on, and can be counted on to be organized and get things done. Often it is the person closest to the situation/ to the one who needs care. The Captain must step up, be

aware and present, and call the shots. On the outside, the
Team Captain appears to be organized and efficient. On the
inside, he or she often feels lonely, scared, and tired.

- **Researcher:** When a new situation or crisis arises, a great
  deal of information must be gathered. Circumstances,
  experience, and evidence are part of every situation; caregiving is no different. Much is to be learned, many things
  need to be investigated, and various ways to accomplish a
  task must be acquired. The Researcher becomes the family
  librarian of information.

- **Questioner:** With an array of new people; a mountain of
  articles to read; medications to learn about; a new normal
  to be developed; and the need for physical, emotional, and
  mental care; doctors to coordinate; and home help care
  to source, there will always be numerous unknowns. One
  needs to ask many questions and find specific and the best
  answers. This role is almost one of a consultant.

- **Helper:** Each role will need assistance at different times.
  Not everyone can do everything all the time. But everyone can do something some of the time. The roles shift,
  and the one who steps in for a special task or time is in an
  important role. The list of how the help is delivered is long:
  helping with confinement, making travel possible, getting
  through post-surgery, and more. The Helper can go from
  distant Cheerleader to hands-on and back again. On the
  inside, they feel satisfied and know they have done what
  they could. They also sometimes feel inadequate compared
  with others.

- **Distant Cheerleader:** Not all healing is hands-on. Some takes place at a distance. Distant Cheerleaders can make phone calls, write e-mails and letters, offer financial support, and provide a different kind of healing that is a valuable addition to what is happening onsite. Some send packages and others provide conversation about subjects different from the daily caregiving topics. Reports about grandchildren and activities in different parts of the family and in different parts of the country provide a diversion and expand the caree's confined world.

Feelings and emotions are the glue that bonds many caregivers and carees. When observing, listening, and sharing, they find they share many of the same feelings—just for different reasons. When their sharing takes place in an honest and loving space, everybody wins and everyone does better.

Family is one of the most difficult systems to navigate. It is also true that the stresses of caregiving can be connected as a cause or a result of other systems. Studying those systems can be like opening a can of worms.

As a child, living near Wood Lake, I used to go fishing for bullheads with my dad. I learned quickly to put a worm on a hook. What was difficult for me was to get the worm out of the can. Now they come in cups, but back then they came in cans similar to a tuna can. Once open, there was a mess of wriggling worms. They were intermingled, and it was hard to grab just one. Navigating the disorganized, slippery mass of worms was difficult. Though the can was full of individual worms, they wrapped around one another. Some clustered in an enmeshed mess. Eventually, through patient effort, I could sort one out, bait my hook, and finally fish.

In all the intertwined needs and changes that arise in a caregiver-caree situation, my awareness is how many feelings and needs are similar for both the caree and the caregiver. When viewed as one person with all the needs, the caree, and another with all the responsibility, the caregiver, it feels lonely and burdensome. However, when the two honestly share their feelings, it turns into an opportunity and possibility. That holds true for the team members as well. When sharing and connection take place—caregivers to caree and caregivers to caregivers—the team comes together and healing takes place.

My dear mentor, Virginia Satir, called this time "the time of reckoning." Ultimately, she believed that all relationships are one-to-one. Sibling to sibling, parent to child, child to parent, and partner to partner. Her experience taught her that in the best of times only one in ten families are able to put together a mixture of two-way relationships. That would be the happy and healthy relationship. The more members who can join the tribe or the core, the happier and healthier each family system.

MY FAMILY AS A CAREGIVING TEAM

Caregiving and care receiving has been a part of our family system for some time. You have read about my experience of the care I received from many paid and unpaid caregivers. At this point I want to look more closely at the experience my children and spouse had as caregivers. They stepped in to help with the care I needed in my home. I have been fortunate to have my team, as there has been and is help available from all of my children.

The day-to-day response came from my son, Pat. He lives nearby and stepped in whenever urgent and steady care was needed. He became the Team Captain the moment he received the call from my soul mate, Joe, with the news that I had fainted and fallen down the stairs. One of my daughters, Sandy, is a professional caregiver and has been since she was a teen. Her advice has been invaluable. She became a Researcher as well as a Distant Cheerleader. My other daughter, Deb, became a hands-on Helper as well as a Distant Cheerleader. She showed up and stepped in when day-to-day and specific help was needed.

Another important member of the team was filled by one of my grandsons and his wife. It just so happened that he had planned a multiday trip, his first lengthy vacation from his job, when he heard of my incident. Immediately, he and his wife changed plans and flew to Colorado. They were in my kitchen making dinner when I came home from rehab—in intense pain—on my walker. They stayed, loved us, and brought us into a new phase of healing. He and his wife were Helpers and Cheerleaders.

Another group that made my recovery possible was my inner circle of friends. My cupboards and bedroom door were covered in cards, and flowers and plants sat on pieces of furniture. All emitted love and each helped heal me. One friend sent a card every week for a year. If you know someone who is ill or injured, take the time to write and send a note to them. This is caring for them. It matters. Be a team member, welcome all team members, and appreciate every team member. It's the only way for true healing to occur.

My children and soul mate have been and remain the core of my immediate caregiving team. My soul mate never left my side at the hospital or missed a day visiting me in rehab, even though he was dealing with his own challenges. And my invaluable children, who are siblings as well as teammates, provided urgent and immediate care, professional advice, and hands-on care from a distance while lifting my spirit with their presence and words. They have their own thoughts and feelings. I am grateful that they shared their experience about being part of a caregiving family team. I've asked them to speak for themselves.

PAT

When I received the call from Joe, my stepdad, that my mother had suffered a back injury from a fall down the stairs and was at the hospital, a chill went through me. I was immediately concerned as to how serious it was. By the time my stepdad had called, she had been taken by ambulance and admitted to our local hospital. I immediately went there with my niece and her friend, who were visiting my mom. We saw that she was in pain and needed many tests and X-rays to determine the extent of the damage.

I talked to the nurses and, eventually, her doctor to learn what the next steps were going to be. They had a conservative option for a back brace, which my mom tried on for a fitting and immediately knew that it was not feasible. The other option was for a surgery that had shown good results. After talking with Mom and Joe, she decided on the surgery. Luckily, the surgery was performed quickly and she responded well to it.

All along I had been speaking with my sisters and my mom's friends to keep everyone updated. Mom made a list of everyone she wanted to be informed about her status, so I created an e-mail list, letters, and a communication plan to keep everyone informed so she could focus on getting well.

Then came rehabilitation. The hardest part for me was having to quickly research options, which included an inpatient rehab center or home health care assistance. My sister is a nurse, so she provided good input regarding what kind of care facility was best for Mom. We picked one we thought would work. My mom had a strong desire to go home upon discharge from the hospital, but with her husband being over eighty-five and their living in a two-story home, I felt it was too risky for both of them and pushed for the rehab transition option, to be followed by in-home physical therapy. Ultimately, that is what Mom opted to do.

The hardest part of the ordeal from my perspective was when the medical transport came to take her to the rehab unit directly from the hospital. She was crying nonstop and looked so frail and sad as they loaded her into the van to go to the center. I really wondered if we had done the right thing. I followed behind the van with my stepdad, and upon arrival, we checked her into the facility.

With my sister's input, I had researched three facilities nearby that had space if and when Mom might need it. After consulting with a local resource who is a hospice nurse, we had picked the one that was best reviewed. Mom received good physical treatment there and had a private room. She was very unhappy, however, with the quality of care by the staff in the evenings, so we hired additional caregivers to literally sleep on the floor next to her bed in the evening.

During this process, she needed items from home, such as clothing and computer gear, and visits to help stay focused on her recovery. My stepdad cannot drive, so I took him there sometimes. He used Uber to visit her there as well. In talking to Mom while she was at the rehab center, she was able, with the rehab coordinator, to make up lists of what her needs were both at the center and once she got back home. I went through them all and tried to make sure she had the support she needed to get stronger. That included having medical equipment, such as a bed, walker, and tub seat, purchased and installed at her house prior to her return.

Joe and I met with staff nurses, a social worker, and the director of the rehab center to relay concerns she had over meal deliveries, responsiveness of staff to her needs, and issues with a wandering patient at the facility who would enter her room at night. Her concerns made me feel terribly guilty, as I had done so much work to find what I had thought was the right facility, but it was not going well. I had done the best I could in the immediate moment to find a spot for her and to make the transition back to being at home as smooth as possible. It was much rockier than I would have liked.

We later determined that even with her bad experience there, it was likely that other rehab centers were worse. The physical therapy helped, and when she returned home, the in-home care staff were very helpful.

Mom was relieved to be back home and was very good about doing her physical therapy as well. We addressed additional ongoing practical matters once she was back home, including nutritional meal plans, home health care aides, transportation, and installing a gate to block the stairs so she would not have a repeat incident.

Throughout this process, I became aware of how quickly things could change. We had all been out to dinner with her granddaughter and family the evening before, and then, *BAM!* the accident happened that same night. I was grateful my stepfather was there and was able to get help and arrange for her to get to the ER as quickly as he did. He also stayed right by her bed and slept at the hospital when she was admitted so she did not have to be alone.

The accident changed some things for them both permanently. They travel less since the accident, and they now have a rotating group of caregivers for in-home care, house cleaning, meal preparation, and making ride arrangements.

Aging is something that we will all experience (God willing), and I have learned the importance of pre-planning for as many unforeseen "events" as is reasonably possible.

To that end, I attended a caregiver class with her that our local agency on aging offered. I learned more about the whole caregiving process. I also accept that some things you cannot plan for, and the ability to react—quickly, in person, and as calmly as possible—can make a big difference for the whole family. I am relieved Mom did so well, and am grateful that I was able to be here for her to help her through a dark time.

DEB

When I got the phone call that Mom had taken a fall, I had been running errands in town. Arriving back into my car, I noticed I had a missed call on my phone and a voicemail from a family member who lives near Mom. Immediately, I was concerned that there was an emergency. My stepdad had been battling several health issues at the time, and my first thought was that he had a problem. I was surprised to hear that it was Mom who had the emergency.

The family member who called me was very calm and logical, which is what I needed at the time. I live thousands of miles away from my mom, so I was very thankful that my brother lived closer and was able to be right there with her. It would have been much more frightening for her if she had to go through that without any family member nearby. If that had been the case, then one of us siblings would have had to somehow get there immediately to be there for her.

I wasn't able to speak with Mom right away, but my family members who were there were very good about calling me to keep me updated on the situation. As soon as I was able, I spoke with my mom. I could tell she was overwhelmed with everything, with lots of emotions.

I wanted to know how she was doing, but I also know that it is hard for someone undergoing a personal crisis to always keep everyone updated, so it was nice that my brother was on location and was very good about keeping me up-to-date.

After the initial crisis, discussions ensued regarding plans for dealing with longer-term issues. I appreciated that my brother was there to help Mom make the transition from the medical caregiving location back to her home. Lots of things had to be set up and in place to make that happen.

Once Mom was home and started her longer-term care, we had more discussions about how my sister and I could also help. My older sister, a nurse, has great knowledge and experience with long-term care for the elderly. I felt thankful that she would be able to advise my mom on those aspects. A lot is involved with that, and much of it concerns things I wouldn't know about.

Of course, if none of us had necessary expertise, we would have had to research it, but it was helpful that my sister already had much experience in that area. I wasn't able to be on the scene immediately and had no experience with elder-care planning, but I was able to offer what I could. And that was to be there in person, help clean, cook, and run errands. Basically just be there. After raising five kids in a remote location far away from family, that kind of hands-on help was what I could offer.

I was able to fly down to be with Mom for a week. One area of concern I had was her ability to eat properly following the injury. I took an inventory of groceries on hand and organized food cupboards and the pantry. I planned some menus and headed off to the grocery store. Raising five kids has led me to pay close attention to nutrition, so I tried to get healthy and nutritious foods. I cooked meals for the week I was there, and I also cooked some meals in advance that I froze, to be eaten after I left. I was able to run some errands to local stores.

Another thing I was able to do was to share in some fun activities. One thing we enjoyed together was watching BBC TV shows in the evening—while eating ice cream! Having this distraction was helpful for Mom during this time.

I do wish I lived closer. I would love to be able to help provide nutritious meals more regularly, but I offered and did what I could.

I remember feelings of concern over the immediate medical crisis, and then feeling thankful that my brother was able to be right there at the crucial immediate time. I was also grateful that my sister had the background and expertise with elder care that she does. That made me feel like I didn't have to know everything, and that I could concentrate on what I did know. This is how we made a good team to be there for Mom.

SANDY

When my mom fell, I was going through a difficult time with many important things going on in my life. When I received the call that my mom had fallen down the stairs and was taken to the emergency room, I was very scared for her and wished that I lived closer so that I could be there with her.

I was thankful that my brother lived near my mom and that he could be at the hospital to support her and my stepdad. He was helpful in advocating for her, and provided us with information on her condition and plan of care. I called my mom daily and offered support while she was in the hospital. She told me that she appreciated my calls and hearing my voice. She updated me on her pain levels, her fear, and her emotional overwhelm with having to accept care from others.

I have thirty-five years of experience as a registered nurse and nursing care manager. I felt like I was able to provide both practical and emotional support. When it was time for decisions to be made about whether to discharge her to home or to a facility for additional rehabilitation, I attempted to give her my input and educate her about her options. I wished I could have been hands-on, but my role grew into a consulting one rather than being part of the daily team. I wanted to be present at her bedside but wasn't able to.

After my mom transferred to the rehabilitation center, I continued to call her daily to receive updates on her condition and offer my love and support. My daily life continued to be demanding in its own way. I was thankful when my nephew and his wife and my sister were able to stay with my mom following her discharge from the rehabilitation facility. They were able to provide emotional support as well as hands-on shopping and cooking. I was also thankful that my mom could become connected with daily professional support to help with physical therapy, occupational therapy, and medication management. I could hear some hope coming back into my mom's voice, and I knew she was healing.

My mom and I have both been on a healing journey in the past year. I continue to have concerns about icy sidewalks at their home. A fall could be so critical. I have asked my mom to consider options to reducing this risk. She has so far continued to want to live at home. I have informed her that I am willing to help explore resources and support decision making going forward, but I will wait and see what she and my stepdad decide about that.

JOE

Our townhouse has a two-level stairway with eight steps in the lower level and nine more steps to the upper level. During an episode with COPD, I had moved from the upstairs bedroom to the lower guest bedroom with my oxygen machine, which is quite noisy. I suddenly heard a major vibrating crash somewhere in the house. I thought it might have even come from the neighbor's house, which is attached to ours. I ran out to the foot of the stairs to see Sharon lying upside down on the upper landing, unable to move. I ran up to her but resisted the urge to try to lift her.

I left her lying there while I called 911 for help. I heard myself saying a prayer. I'm eighty-seven years old and was scared to death.

I also called Sharon's son, Pat. He responded immediately. Both the ambulance and Pat arrived very quickly.

The county rescue crew loaded her very smoothly onto their stretcher and headed for Boulder Community Hospital emergency room. An ultrasound examination revealed a compression fracture in her lumbar spine. Sharon had a broken back.

They wanted to admit her, but no beds were available at the moment. So she had to remain in the emergency room bed until a room became available. I stayed with her, sleeping on a too-short, not-padded-enough window seat for three nights. It was the only place I wanted to be. Sharon has been my most devoted caregiver; now it was my turn to be hers.

When Pat arrived, we instantly became a team, both caring for Sharon. Our relationship deepened, and we knew we would be close forever for having shared this trauma and the need for caregiving.

It was lonely without Sharon in our home, and the hardest part was going home to an empty house. I walked through all the motions of caring for myself when I realized that everything had changed. I breathed a huge sigh of relief with the professional caregivers who came to our home to care for Sharon (and indirectly, me), as our house was full of professional caregivers for several weeks. Today the feeling is still gratitude.

BRIDGE BUILDING

We build too many walls and
not enough bridges.

—Isaac Newton

The idea of building bridges in caregiving crystallized when
I felt disconnected and angry because I could not make my
smart TV do what I wanted it to do. Having considered myself
smart, discerning, and capable, I felt defeated. How could this be
happening to me?

I turned to my tech-savvy son for help. He showed up in his
personal/professional way with a chart, care, and instructions. He
walked me through my "old" way of viewing the TV: recording,
choosing, and watching. He then instructed me in the "new" way
of understanding how smart TVs work and how to easily enjoy
the many choices my up-to-date TV offered. Then he continued
to coach me.

In essence, he built a bridge. And that inspired a leap in my thinking about the many ways we can build bridges. For a while, all I could see in our current culture was isolation and problems. Now I can see bridges and possibilities. That was a whole new and bigger way of looking at issues in our lives that can overwhelm us:

- information overload in the workplace
- long work hours
- difficulty with time management
- technology overload
- caretaking
- choices

It's staggering to think of the number of situations and relationships that need bridge building. Many people are overwhelmed in their personal/professional lives regarding caregiving, such as the following:

- people in need of care
- agencies that provide care
- hospitals
- medical professionals
- families

My position is twofold. I live in a community of people who have found ways to navigate both their professional and personal choices to bring to their lives a sense of order, pleasure, manageability, and quality. They have discovered tools and options that guide them during times of caregiving and needing care.

My second position is that more than enough information is available, as well as willing individuals to lend a hand to aid in understanding and applying the information. What we are short of is bridges that help both the person in need and the caregiver. Working and living with bridges is much more efficient in the long run than everyone building their own empires. There have always been—and always will be—empires in which one person or a group of people establish and maintain control over many others. This is not a judgment; rather, it is a call to build bridges between the tsunami of people in need and those attempting to fill the need.

Whether you are forty years old or over ninety or somewhere in between, your life is changing every day. Change brings opportunities, loss, sadness, fear, love, and responsibility. You may love someone who is also going through great changes. If you add a health diagnosis or illness or an accident to the mix, feeling overwhelmed may be amplified.

Changes affect not only the individual but also the people in that person's life, including the caregivers and loved ones. The need for care is mushrooming, involving millions of people taking care of others—without remuneration. Also a large number of paid professionals and agency workers, and more people are joining the ranks of caregivers every day. Countless books, blogs, websites, articles, and podcasts are available to provide information about caregiving. Conferences are springing up in all these fields. Two of the best and the largest are the Annual National Caregiving Conference and the Family Caregiver's Alliance, yet we have the persistent problem of caregivers and carees feeling overwhelmed and that the help they need, particularly during a crisis, is out of reach.

Maybe it's time to take a deep breath . . . and then a few more, check out your surroundings, discover who within your reach needs help, offer that help, and find your special purpose. Your reward is inner peace, contentment, and wisdom in knowing how and why the world is unfolding in the way it is. You might as well enjoy "now," because now is all there ever is.

As I gave away some furniture to a man I had just met, he said something that has stayed with me. "If we could all take care of the one-hundred feet around us and the twenty closest people in our lives, the world would be a better place. Maybe it's time to stop weighing options, choosing the best route, calculating our own interests, wearing ourselves out, running as fast as we can, answering every phone call, answering each ding on the computer, and so on."

These are tough times in our world. Let's reframe that reality and do what we can to make our world better without losing ourselves in the process. Examine your life, your family, your work, and identify what overwhelms you. Then assess what more you can do or what you can change to make this world a better place to live.

My purpose in writing this book is to frame two things: A simpler way to distill information and not to get lost in words. Just a simpler way to live. How old will you be ten years from now? No matter what your age, what do you want between now and then? It's up to you.

> "I rarely saw my Grandma Markle,
> as she hailed from New Hampshire and spent
> much of her life in Pennsylvania and Florida. To bridge that gap,
> she would always send scrapbooks, care packages and
> boxes of treats made from familiar recipes."
> —Meghan Markle

BRIDGE BUILDING IN THE FAMILY

*"You leave home to seek your fortune, and, when you get it,
you go home and share it with your family."*
—*Anita Baker*

Ideally, the family team would have been built before it's needed in a crisis. However, as we saw in Chapter 6, the team often doesn't come together until the need arises. Every family likely has an informal and unspoken system in place. We have already seen the roles that tend to occur in all family systems, whether Family Friendly or Broken.

Now it's time to look at how family members can build bridges with one another while establishing the team. We do that by building on each member's strengths. Whatever your family role in caregiving, or combination of roles, it is possible to build new bridges among family members when caregiving is needed—to move beyond negativity and disengagement and into support and connection.

Whatever your family role in caregiving, or combination of roles, it is possible to build new bridges among family members when caregiving is needed—to move beyond negativity and disengagement and into support and connection.

Organizing the members' abilities into their natural roles is a much-needed task. Welcome the Team Captain—the lead organizer. Supporting him/her in any way is every member's role. When someone needs to be forceful or questioning, such as when working with scheduling, doctor's offices staff, etc., go to the expert or the Questioner. They can be forceful and demanding while also needing team support. Designate someone to be the family Cheerleader, who works to hold the family system informed and connected. Perhaps a family newsletter is called for. The family member who does not enjoy public contact becomes the perfect Helper and provides the nurturing the caree and the rest of the family need. Every member/role has strengths and handicaps. Bundle this into teamwork and all will benefit.

Practical Tools for Building Bridges in the Family

- Call and e-mail one another.
- Forgive childhood hurts, with or without professional help.
- Look for a support group for yourself.
- Take time for self-nourishment.
- Ask for help.
- Tell your caree the best memories you have.
- Find something in the caree's current life that you can share and cherish with him or her.
- Treat your family as well as you do your friends.
- Share your feelings.
- Be vulnerable with one another.

Recognize that when memory issues or conflicts arise, everyone is under pressure and stress. This is especially true when any kind of dementia, Parkinson's disease, or memory loss is involved. Living with this kind of daily pressure and stress is like caring for a two-year-old. They need 24/7 supervision and care. No one person, or even family, can do it. It takes a team within and often beyond the family.

No one can assure smooth family sailing when people are thrust together in times of need. Just when people need each other most, it's easy for tension to win the day, especially when the crisis needs quick and immediate attention. When changes come gradually, there is more time to plan. It's time for bridge building.

I asked a friend of mine how his relationship was going with his brother since their mother needed more and a different kind of care, which required making several decisions. His answer was interesting and prompted my thinking. He said, "All I have ever wanted was a closer relationship to my brother and now I have it. Interestingly, it was a surprise to find it's not what I really wanted. My brother is rigid, angry, and critical. We came from the same family, but now, as adults, we have nothing in common. We came from the same mother and father but are not alike in ways that matter. I am much closer to a friend."

In the unsettled times of caring for a family member, events can be full of information and clarity. Every event or issue is an opportunity to view it from different perspectives. Some families are splintered even more in crisis, and others pull together and strengthen ties. Sometimes divorce, hard words, and distance will take the family to a new level of strain, shattering some families even more. Others will use the occasion to grow closer, to forgive, and to start anew.

As we reach certain ages (forty is one accepted age), we often seem to reflect on broken relationships and attempt reconciliation. Life after sixty is another point when we consider the possibility of reconciling relationships. How would any of us as family members try to find that last grasp at the golden ring of personal satisfaction, connections, and fulfillment? It may be that "bridge building" is the pathway.

My friend Ann was diagnosed with metastatic breast cancer and told she would not win the battle against it. Within two weeks, her

four daughters and two sons formed a care team and helped their
mother on her journey. One of them, an executive in another city,
put together a plan for the family to follow. Two of Ann's children
helped her move into a condo from her home, and the other two
took turns staying with her. The other child handled interfacing
with doctors, home health care, and, in the end, hospice. Ann lived
eight months from diagnosis to death, and it perhaps was some of
the best months of her life because her family pulled together as
a team. She died with dignity and inner peace.

Many people wonder if something like this could ever happen
to the people in their families. But one will never know until put
to the test or, better, until the family discusses ahead of time what
their plan might be should one of them be in crisis and need care.

MORE PRACTICAL TOOLS FOR THE WHOLE FAMILY

1. **Make a "first call for help" resource book.** The phone
   numbers need to be displayed or put into a phone.
2. **Keep a list or an address book of all close friends.** This
   list needs to include their phone numbers. This circle of
   friendship will become increasingly important as to who
   to notify of anything related to the caree. Some people
   keep an inner circle group list in their contacts. Update
   the list once a year.
3. **Keep all medications (dosage amounts and times)
   posted in the room of the caree.** This list should be visi-
   ble to all family members, emergency transport, hospital
   emergency rooms, or urgent care. It is good to keep this
   list with driver's license or identification card posted in a
   private room in the caree's home. It needs to be updated

each time there is a change in medication, and copies
should be given to the people who would be involved in
"first call for help."

4. **Clean all kitchen cupboards of what is not necessary.**
   Move the "in use" items to the front of the cupboards and
   keep only what is necessary. Reaching in and lifting from
   cupboards is often difficult and somewhat dangerous.
   Keep what gets regularly used. Give away or sell what is
   no longer needed. It can be replaced if necessary.

5. **Check the house for safety needs.** Throw rugs should be
   removed. Falls account for a large majority of the admis-
   sions to rehabilitation centers. Also be aware of foot-
   stools or any other things that can be tripped over. Make
   sure that nothing is stored on steps.

6. **Declutter.** I define clutter as anything lying around with
   no use or order. In my home, I subscribe to the adage "my
   clutter is my memories." Therefore, I have one room that
   I refer to as my meditation room, museum, and keeper
   of my memories. Everything is a gift or a handmade
   item I cannot part with. I once worked in a church that
   practiced palanca, which is a Spanish word that loosely
   means "a tangible form of spiritual energy." My *palanca*
   room is full of treasures. While I cannot part with them,
   my family will be able to someday. They may divide some
   of the treasures among family and friends. The rest they
   can throw away, as they do not have the same attachment to the items as I do. All my other rooms are fairly
   clutter-free. I keep one wall of one room for family and
   memory photos. Again, someday someone in the family

may want one and the rest can be digitalized or thrown out—easier for my family to do than for me.

7. **Find a way to declutter your memories as well.** If you can tell your stories through photos or the written word, or verbalize them in family meetings or gatherings, then it will be available to anyone in the family who wants to know their history. Some care, some don't. Yet in my long history of working as a family therapist, each person wonders at some time in their life who they are, where they came from, and how they are connected to history and to one another. If you keep everything, no one will figure it out. If the information is distilled and distributed in an easy and simple way, you'll share more history.

8. **Enjoy—enjoy—enjoy.** Enjoy one another while you have one another. Tell family stories and highlight the fun times. Try to forgive and forget the rest. Life is so short and sometimes catches us off guard. Be as ready as you can for what may come. Living this way is a kindness you give to those around you.

ENJOY EVERYTHING YOU CAN

9. **Face the hard things, and talk about them.** It will be easier for your family to face crisis and change if you have developed the habit of discussing matters such as finances, independence, and death. Other difficult subjects we have already mentioned, such as when to stop driving and when and how to downsize.

10. **Finances is one of the hardest subjects to talk about.** It's often the issues around financial matters that cause the deepest wounds. How is a financial trustee chosen? What are the criteria one uses when making plans, and when is the plan to be put into place? Here again is another place where teamwork comes into play. Among the many ways to leave a legacy, financial planning is one of them, including choosing the trustee of valuable items belonging to the caree.

11. **A final role is a legacy trustee, who safeguards and transmits the history and value system of the person.** In a well-working family system, different people in the family will likely take on the responsibilities of articulating and passing on the different parts of the caree's life.

SUMMARY FOR FAMILY BRIDGE BUILDING

- Decide to share the load as a family.
- Visit the caree as often as possible.
- Heal old wounds, forget some, and start over again.
- Show appreciation as often as you can.
- Learn the art of storytelling.
- Share feelings and build authentic relationships.

- Review the good times in the family through photos.
- Touch the people you love in affectionate ways.

BRIDGE BUILDING WITH YOURSELF

"The most common way people give up their power
is by thinking they don't have any."
—*Alice Walker*

Most of us know when we've reached a time in our lives when our
way of doing something goes dry, and we feel like we don't have
anything left inside. Then we struggle with ourselves, and fatigue
and fear can take over.

We have come to know that all the information in the world
isn't necessarily going to fix our situation; sometimes it becomes
a new problem. The search for balance and self-care is a process of
making choices between the bad and the good, then between the
good and the better, and finally the ones that work for us: the best
of the best. We begin to build choice and change into our future.
We accept that life isn't set in stone. It's ever changing. In all areas
of our lives we will have questions and roadblocks, possibilities
and opportunities. We simply need to plug in and take what we
need for ourselves.

Simple Tools for Self-Care

- **Eat a good breakfast.** Every dietician and doctor say this, but often we don't
  do it. Picture a stove, furnace, or fireplace. It starts working in the morning only
  when fuel is added. We gas up the car so it can function. Our bodies are the same

way. We have to stoke the furnace or fill the tank. Choose two of your favorite, nutritious, and easy-to-prepare breakfasts. Always have the ingredients on hand. Then you never have to think much about what you'll have for breakfast.

- **Take a walk.** It doesn't matter when. You can do one long walk or break it into many ten-minute walks throughout the day. You will respond better psychologically and physically. Read *Calmer Waters: The Caregiver's Journey Through Alzheimer's and Dementia* for inspiration.

- **Sleep with aromatherapy oil fragrance.** Eucalyptus is maybe the best sleep inducer, with lavender a close second. Put a drop of oil on cotton balls and breathe in their relaxation and calmness before going to bed. It works wonders and ensures better sleep.

- **Stay in the here and now.** "You'd better enjoy the here and now, because it's going to be 'now' for the rest of your life." Make every hour count, and don't waste any time on negativity or worry about the past or the future.

- **Sing and dance.** Commuting is a great opportunity to sing along with the radio. As I have been aging, I have found that my voice was getting softer, and often people would ask me to repeat what I said. After a few months of singing in the car, my voice has begun projecting again and has regained its strength.

Adopt a pet—but only if you have the time and the agility to be around a pet. However, if your work is such that you do not do hands-on caregiving and spend a great deal of time with a computer or isolating behavior, a pet might be just the right comfort for you. This is a very personal decision.

- **Laugh.** Find the humor in daily situations. It's all around us when we look for it. Even with years of caregiving, humor is found in many situations. Find it. It's like a vein of gold. If you have to watch old movies or TV shows that make you laugh, it's worth it. Many documented studies are available about the healing aspect of humor. Look for books and shows by Norman Cousins. His work on "laughing yourself well" is well researched and documented.

- **Grow something.** Watching life grow is nourishing and life-giving. It might be a small garden. If space is tight, just a few container pots. Don't forget herbs. Carees often lose their sense of taste, so fresh herbs become a treat. If it's too much work, get a houseplant and nurture yourself by having something green and beautiful in your surroundings.

- **Develop an attitude of gratitude.** How lucky we are to share a close relationship to our carees! Whether it's family or client intimacy, closeness and trust are feelings not everyone gets to experience in this life. Find the gratitude in yourself, and the relationships to the people in your life will take on deeper meaning and give great contentment and joy. Purpose is one of the higher gifts of life, and you discover what that truly means as a caregiver.

- **Evaluate your space.** Do you hang out, or do you have space that feeds your soul? It may be color, it might be a meditation room, or it could be simply one pillow that lifts and feeds your heart and soul. Fresh flowers, a few pillows, colors that soothe, iced tea, or hot chocolate readily available all have calming and soothing qualities. Listen to soothing music. Make your home your sanctuary; it will go a long way toward preventing burnout.

- **Find a support group.** Caregivers often tell their carees to seek a support group while ignoring their own need for support as well . . . and sometimes even more so. Many support groups are available, and each caregiver needs to have one.

"A day without humor is a day wasted."
—Charlie Chaplin

BRIDGES BETWEEN FRIENDS

"Many people will walk in and out of your life, but only
true friends will leave footprints in your heart."
—Eleanor Roosevelt

As we navigate this job of growing older, we change and life changes. We keep some friends, we lose some friends, and all connections change in important ways. Each age and each era has friends. When we're young, they're playmates. As teens, buddies or BFFs. As adults, we use the word *friends*, and as we age, perhaps *companions* is the better descriptive. All it means is that we share important parts of ourselves with others. Since we are ever changing, it is no wonder that we have many different friends and friendships throughout our lifetime.

Some friends are transient, with us only a short while. Yet their impact lasts forever, either in fact or in memory. Some friends are what I call Silver Friends. They are the friends we are very close to at a particular time in life—high school or college classmates, military comrades, or neighbors. The time with them was so rich that we can pick right up where we left off and never skip a beat, regardless of the many years between connections.

Another group I call Golden Friends. These are the people we never lose touch with. They are here and now. We stay in regular contact in person, by telephone, e-mail, or Skype. They are part of our daily living, whether they are close by or far away. This is our inner circle. I am in regular contact with my Golden Friends. (My inner circle list is on my emergency contact list.)

People don't tend to die from failure to thrive or old age. They often die of loneliness and lack of connection. Making friends starts as toddlers and continues over the decades. Some friends we have known since day care and we have chosen to keep these friendships alive. Friendships are like plants and any living thing. They need food and nourishment to thrive. Friendships are a matter of choice.

In my earlier work and writing, I often referred to friends as "families of choice." As our lives change, and we change with it, time, distractions, and interests help us sort out who we let into our inner circle at any time. As we navigate the series of dilemmas life brings, we stay in touch about the real and authentic things happening in our lives, not just the happy times.

A dear professional colleague who travels a great deal told me once that she met someone on a two-hour plane ride. They became instant friends and have been communicating now for more than fifteen years. They are Golden Friends, though they have met in person only twice. Another colleague also met someone on an airplane, talked over a stress incident during the flight, and this person's attitude changed her life forever. This fellow traveler was an acquaintance, never to be contacted again, but a part of her soul was healed forever because of this encounter.

Differences in living situations, divorce, jobs, interests, politics, belief systems, disagreements, and a host of other reasons can cause some friends to drift apart, change the status of the friendship, or end the relationship. Maybe this doesn't apply to you, but then again maybe it does. Do you need to build any bridges between friends? Do you need to resume these friendships, or let some go? Do you want to contact anyone and check out the current involvement and investment in that friendship? Think over your life and the people in it. Do some self-searching and check out the quality and connection in those friendships. Sometimes bridge building is exactly what you want to do.

It's within our grasp to seek out people to share our life energy with while expecting them to share their energy with us. With true friends, sometimes it's a quiet connection, while sometimes it's noisy laughter. No true friendship includes pressure but always learning and wisdom.

Choose friends wisely. Who plans for the future? Who thinks about these kinds of issues, who is setting up resources and finances for lifelong caring? Is this someone I can count on when I need support and help? Are there people I could share a home and a life with more easily than other people? Some are very willing to look at reality and the needs of change, while many are not. Those with the attitude of "I will worry when I need to," or, "I am working hard to live in the present," or, "The government should take care of me" are going to have a rude awakening when the first crisis hits. You will want friends who encourage self-care and self-appreciation.

CONDUCTING A FRIENDSHIP INVENTORY

Friendship is a major connection in life. We are whole people, and whenever we connect a part of ourselves to another person, we build a bridge. The more parts of ourselves we develop, the more chances we have to meaningfully connect with others. The way to do a friendship inventory is to ask, "What area of interest have I developed that someone else would be interested in pursuing with me?"

After conducting a friendship inventory, this is what I came up with:

- **Physical:** Kate is my friend who likes to walk as much as I do. A few days a week, we go on "our" walk. This time together is fun, it's interesting, it's dependable, and we both stay healthier.
- **Emotional:** When I need to vent or share my frustrations and happiness, I call Jane. She laughs with me; she cries with me. We live in different states, but we feel connected to each other's daily life because we talk and share in an emotional and authentic way. She is like a happy relationship with a sister. Another friend, Ken, also makes me laugh. He has a sense of humor and great stories. He is like seasoning in my life.
- **Mental:** Janet and I are both thinkers, creative, and love to explore ideas. Our way of staying connected is to read the same book at the same time. Since she lives in another state, our friendship could drift if we didn't find a way to keep it alive, relevant, and happy. We schedule a talk once a month.
- **Social:** Kirsten and I like doing things together. We both love to visit art galleries and try out new restaurants. We are "doer" friends, and when something fun comes up, she is the one I call to see if she is interested.
- **Spiritual:** I share the same fellowship with Laurie. We love to talk, share, and explore possibilities together.

I walk with Kate, cry and share with Jane, have long philosophical talks with Janet, go places with Kirsten, and explore myself with Laurie. Some friends, like Jim, may cover multiple areas. He has been a friend for forty years. Jim knows me, my family, my wants, my worries, and my needs. He is very smart and guides me as well. I share a closeness with all my friends whom I cherish. Today I have fewer casual friends. I really don't have time to waste, so each friendship is a major value to me.

My fortune is great because of many of my family members, partner, and business associates are also dear and trusted friends. My cup runneth over. Parties, dinners, and gatherings are always possibilities for making a new friend. However, time and inner peace are factors, and it's very hard to keep up several friendships.

BRIDGE BUILDING WITH PETS

"Until one has loved an animal, a part of one's soul remains unawakened."
—Anatole France

Do not underestimate the power of animals to enrich the lives of the caregiver and the caree. Animals give and receive love. They have the power to help one lower blood pressure, release relaxation hormones, oxytocin and serotonin, and cut down on stress hormones. Ultimately pets:

- make us feel supported;
- make us feel less lonely;
- give us purpose;
- are fun to love;

- teach us great lessons;
- provide companionship; and
- help us discover more emotions.

Dogs, cats, rabbits, hamsters, guinea pigs, birds, and even horses often become family members. Even the very different and less common pets such as ferrets and iguanas can trigger wonderful memories and attachments. It is no accident that many people now use trained "therapy dogs" in their healing process and their effort to lead a healthier, healing lifestyle.

In my lifetime, I have known many dogs in our family. I will probably forget one, but these are the ones that readily come to mind: Skeeter, Pudgie, Blackie, Tashia, Pepper, Toby, Trixie, BJ, Daisy, Maggie, Kayla, Runty, Jack, Boo, Oreo, Nickii, Snoopy, Ginger, Jake, Lucy, Mindy, Caper, Molly, Chena, Scottie, Snoopy, and Scout. They are part of not only our family history but also our present.

One time when we went back to the small town in Minnesota where I grew up to visit my aunt and my children's great-aunt, we were surprised that another visitor in her care center was a goat. The little goat had just been born and brought back dozens of memories of the many years my aunt lived on a farm and knew the cycle of life through animals. We all, including the baby goat, made her day.

In my rehab center after my fall, I couldn't have visitors. The hours were long, and how I longed for the "former me" when I spent many hours walking with my son's dog, Molly. One day, Molly came prancing into my room. My heart danced. Knowing the hospital had occasional therapy dogs brought in, my son walked Molly in (he didn't stop to ask permission), and she spent precious time with me. Between two friends posing as my spiritual directors and our family dog coming to visit, joy and hope returned.

The joy and the lessons pets afford in our lives cannot be measured, and each one's departure leaves a hole in our hearts. Meanwhile, we love them and they love us. They are great caregivers and healers.

BRIDGES IN MEDICAL CARE

"I've learned that people will forget what you said, people will forget what you did, but people will never forget how you make them feel."
—*Maya Angelou*

Once a physical or mental crisis or a medical problem is established, the next step is to seek help with professional care.

When the crisis is sudden, the sequence often includes a call to 911, ambulance service, emergency rooms, hospitalization, and often rehabilitation and physical therapy. Oftentimes it's a new experience for a family system, so they don't know where to begin. One would think it should just all fall into place. It does not. Many decisions need to be made quickly: which hospital, which doctors to call, whether or not to authorize surgery, how to close up the house, where to get clothes, and how to get bedside needs met. If another caree is at home, there is another set of decisions. Who will take care of that person, and provide transportation, food, medication, and supervision? This is a major crisis for the family system.

The crisis does not end with hospitalization or rehabilitation. It continues with the transition back home. The whole experience starts over. Transportation home, food, clothing, and shelter needs, medication management, sometimes mobility and transportation issues. It all takes time, willingness to attend to details, and money. When there is too little, what happens?

Care very often includes a primary doctor, several specialists, a dentist, and any special needs the caree might have. When these participants work together, the best bridges are built. Too often they are not, and care is disjointed, incomplete, and frustrating for all involved—caregivers as well as carees.

RELATIONSHIPS WITH PROFESSIONALS

Both my soul mate and I have had to—and continue to—interact with medical professionals. We also have had doctors and nurses in our family setting as professional paid caregivers in addition to family members as nonpaid caregivers.

It helps to have one person on the family team be the contact person for making appointments, as well as knowing when a doctor's visit is completely private and when it is helpful to have a second set of ears to hear information and to record and keep files. A range of paid caregivers can be used in this capacity, as well as with medical management. The important issue is that one person, perhaps with a backup person, is in charge.

From the doctor's point of view, he or she must move quickly, trying to see as many patients as they can. Both doctor and patient can help each other a great deal by understanding the other's perspective.

PREFERRED PATIENT BEHAVIORS

- Do not wait until off hours to make phone calls, unless it is a true emergency.

- Keep a written list of symptoms, reports, and questions, and recognize the doctor's need to see other patients.
- Be as pleasant as truthfully possible. It's hard for doctors and nurses to see pained and ill individuals all day long.
- Be courteous with office staff. They may have had a bad or difficult day navigating between the professionals they work with and the patients who have needs.
- Smile when it's at all possible.
- Be clear and concise.
- Say thank you.

When I faced cancer, I joined a cancer support group to find the courage to help myself and find resources that could support me and walk this journey with me. Sad to say, the support groups I visited became "doctor bashing" groups. Fortunately, I found one that focused on acceptance and courage. Keep looking until you find the one that meets your needs and expectations.

PREFERRED PROFESSIONAL BEHAVIORS

- Smile and say hello before starting to input information into the computer. One doctor we saw rolled over on a wheeled chair and touched the patient's hand before starting the exam. It was very comforting.
- Deliver hard news in a clear and caring way, but do deliver it. Find ways to talk about rather than avoid those hard subjects of terminal illness and end-of-life issues.
- Listen, listen more, and listen hard for the feelings behind the message or question.
- Smile when it's at all possible.

- Make an authentic connection.
- Make referrals to whatever professional seems appropriate. It's really helpful when doctors know the community well enough to be able to refer to resources that address the whole person and can work with other doctors to create the best possible lifestyle for the patient. It makes a win-win situation. My primary doctor has been in this community for a long time, is very connected with paid and unpaid caregivers, and always has some kind of reference for me when I am seeking help.
- Make a nice atmosphere for the patient, if possible. It is comforting when one goes into an operating room and everyone is joking about the head covers they wear and which music they want to play during surgery. That made me feel more relaxed and safer the several times I went for surgery.

My physical therapists have shared with me that just knowing and respecting one another has helped them decide which of them will work with which patient. They have periodic lunches and din-ners together and learn about one another. It helps them to know which patient would work better with which therapist.

For the twenty-six years that I was a patient of the Mayo Clinic in Rochester, Minnesota, it never ceased to amaze me how the Mayo doctors worked with one another. Referring back and forth, trying everything they could for each individual patient, covering for one another in every way. Just sitting in the cafeteria and watching the respect and sharing that went on among the professionals was healing in itself.

It was clearly a patient-centered operation, and one that deserves study and great respect. The fact that the doctors were on salary and not building personal practices contributed to the cooperation and luxury of having a patient-centered practice. Much can be learned from the Mayo model.

It was clearly a patient-centered operation, and one that deserves study and great respect.

BUILDING BRIDGES IN OUR TROUBLED WORLD

"You may not always have a comfortable life, and you will not always be able to solve all of the world's problems at once, but don't underestimate the importance you can have, because history has shown us that courage can be contagious and hope can take on a life of its own."
—*Michelle Obama*

My intent is to draw awareness to the idea of caregiving connection as a fulfilling goal and that it is hard to be responsible all alone all the time. Teams and families can do more, do it more easily, and do it in less time than any individual can possibly do. Once personal bridges are built, one can take that experience and apply it to bigger systems. My mentor, Virginia Satir, talked often about all meaningful communication being:

- within—with ourselves;
- between—any two people; and
- among—in groups.

We live in a time of shattered communication. Many personal and larger worlds are crumbling because of a lack of authentic communication. We can influence the world in general with healing

We can influence the world in general with healing ourselves, families, systems, and groups, and then taking that healing to our bigger world.

ourselves, families, systems, and groups, and then taking that healing to our bigger world.

Someone once told me that if everyone took very good care of the closest ten people in their lives, everyone would be cared for. An oversimplification, I am sure. However, the concept is worthy of consideration. It is impossible for each of us to become president, serve in our legislature, and change laws. It is equally difficult to be the decision maker for any system and change laws and culture within that system. But we do change

But we do change culture and we change the world when we are available for the people in our path.

culture and we change the world when we are available for the people in our path. We can all become bridge builders, who are always looking forward at every stage of life—and at any age.

AGING IS A SUCCESS STORY

I love living. I love that I'm alive to love my age.
There are many people who went to bed just as I did
yesterday evening and didn't wake up this morning.
I love and feel very blessed that I did.

—Maya Angelou

I t's estimated that people with a positive attitude toward aging and other changes in life, live about seven and a half years longer than those with a negative outlook. The fact is, the elderly are getting smarter, richer, and healthier than ever before. And, of course, they are living longer. While aging is not an illness, the risk of accident and chronic illness increases with age. But that in no way diminishes the accomplishment of longevity. Aging is a success story, and downsizing has become a big part of that story.

Most older people have lived long enough to have accumulated far more than they can ever use. Or save. Some of those possessions are tangible things—furniture, heirlooms, and treasured items. Some are intangibles—relationships, memories, and a sense of richness from living a long life. I sometimes think of downsizing as reducing the tangibles and creating more space for the intangibles.

> "Grow old along with me. The best is yet to be."
> —*Robert Browning*

AGING AND DOWNSIZING

While illness or an accident is often the first step to downsizing living space for many, others start the process long before an event occurs that creates a lifestyle change and thrusts people into either caregiver or caree roles. Downsizing can help you be ready for that event.

When does one reframe his or her living conditions from "giving up something" to "entering a new phase?" Eventually, it becomes difficult for family members and caregivers to see someone in their family struggle to "keep up." This is also true for many disabilities as well as when debilitating accidents occur. When does a caree need to leave his or home to live where the caregivers and family can offer the necessary mental, physical, or emotional help? Looking at the move as a hopeful and exciting time will help the caree adjust to the idea of a new environment. As a caregiver, make caring your priority and don't be a landlord of stuff. It hardly ever gives back. Your caree and family will love you for it.

One of the earliest clues that things are changing is recognizing the need to downsize and eliminate clutter. It's part of the successful aging process—letting go and looking ahead, even when there are far fewer years ahead than behind. People often downsize many times before they settle into their last downsizing. They go from one house to another, from house to condo, from condo to apartment, and on and on. There are many sizes and shapes of home ownership, lease, and rent.

DOWNSIZING AND RIGHTSIZING

Sooner or later, we all discover that "less is best" regarding living space. Less to buy, clean, move around, and take care of. The first time one decides to rightsize is the hardest. Then it gets easier and easier and finally becomes a way of life.

> "Americans spend the first two thirds of their lives accumulating
> stuff and the last third getting rid of it."
> —*Anonymous*

Back in the 1990s, my plan was to age in my then current home in Las Vegas forever. I sold my original company in 1995, and while I still continued to be an author and occasionally facilitate a workshop, my home, and all its fun activities, was to be my focus. I found out that "forever" is a long time. Over the years, I have owned condos, apartments, a co-op, and a number of homes. Quite a feat for someone who didn't have $5,000 to her name in her forties.

I have crammed my spaces, large as well as extremely small, with family heirlooms, stuff I love, handmade articles, and a very large library of hand-signed first edition books. I love my books and my homemade scrapbooks. I have no idea at the moment where all this will go. I do know two things:

1. It's so very hard for me to eliminate or toss any handmade gift for me.
2. It will be so easy for my children to do just that.

I have downsized countless times over the last twenty-five years, selling those same condos and homes. My biggest surprise was how much easier living became once I downsized. The last big move was into a small condo. That was a bit of a shock, and it was the best thing I have ever done. Living in a manageable space is the first best step and allows aging at home to go on for a longer period of time. It took a great deal of downsizing to be able to move into a condo. Should you choose this next big step, following are some things I learned:

1. First, know where you want to go. Know what you are working with in terms of square feet, windows, doors, closets, and kitchen. That is your plan.
2. Second, go from room to room and have everything, and I mean everything, put in the middle of the room. Then walk to the outside of the room and ask yourself:
   - What do I want to give away?
   - What do I want to consign?
   - What do I absolutely have to have?

   Don't forget what's in the garage, the attic, basement, and all closets.

3. Check to see who, if anyone, wants anything and give them a deadline date to pick it up.

4. Have a consignment store pick any furniture or items you want to sell.

5. Pack what you absolutely must have.

I have told my children and grandchildren that if I have anything they want, I will see to it that they have it. So far, few takers. One son asked for an apple crystal piece in memory of the times he worked with us on the computer; another daughter said she has room for only jewelry. Another daughter said she treasures the family memories. I am learning fast and furiously that material possessions aren't love, and I pray that they feel my love in many ways.

When my much younger sister died, it was shocking to remember feelings that came up around many of the possessions that she owned. While I realized and knew at a deep level that no possession is worth any family pain, I found out that objects are an indication of treasure, and how we share our treasures evokes feelings.

I am not talking about monetary value. I am referring to emotional attachment and pain. In my family, there were many feelings around a set of dishes. They were all rekindled when those dishes were left to someone who was *not* expecting them and not to someone who *did* expect them. Those feelings at that time might possibly never be forgotten. There is still emotional pain connected to those dishes.

Memories are attached to objects of treasure. How that plays out is different within each family and relationship. I have a wicker basket of all the treasured cards and letters I have received over the years. My hope is that some child or grandchild will read them once before throwing them out. A lifetime of love and memories is in those cards.

In my downsizings, I have both hired a company to help me and I have done it myself—and some things I still avoid. I have gone through all the options of giving, donating, selling, and consigning. Downsizing might feel overwhelming, so don't do it alone. Good help is available. Use it. Do it before you need it. As we go forward, remember that just about everything in your new home will be smaller—bedrooms, kitchen, closets, storage areas. Be wary of storage lockers. This just postpones what you need to do. Get yourself a "moving therapist." The more you ask for professional advice, the easier it becomes to ask again. Try it one more time. If you hang on to any of your ideas "you always had," ask yourself, "How is this going for me? Is it working in every area of my life?" If not, get advice, bite the bullet, and get going. No time better than the present. Downsizing is very hard, but it is also liberating. We came into this life alone, not bothering ourselves much about our possessions, and we leave the same way.

LOIS'S STORY

Lois is the best planner and organizer I ever met and observed. Lois was always thinking and determined "not to be caught short." She had grown up in a painful family and truly believed a bit of pre-planning helped relationships and families.

One of the things I love about her is that she is always thinking about "what is to come" and takes action in the best interest of everyone she loves. Lois honored them, making sure that they heard from her every birthday, holiday, and celebration. Her envelopes showing up in the mailbox were always welcomed. As she aged,

Lois decided to move closer to a family member so as to be nearby if they needed her or she needed them. Moving out of state was a big deal to her. Moving everything was too hard and too expensive, so she needed to part with many of her collections and beautiful pieces of furniture. As she watched her tap clothes and shoes go, she knew it was the end of an era. She let them go gracefully. She lived in a smaller, more affordable home, and she adjusted and was happy. She garnered my respect and admiration.

This era of her life is filled with many activities. She has a grandson nearby. She also has a granddaughter with special needs who lives in another state. Lois filled her days with new interests. She babysat when the family needed her and offered some vacations to her family. Lois has never looked back and has continued to age gracefully. As time passed, she reconsidered her choices and made another huge move—into an 800-square-foot condo. Again, I've learned so much from her.

More Downsizing Tips

1. Start a new habit. Train yourself to choose one area a day to sort through to donate or recycle. Get ready.
2. Gift items to family and friends now. Have fun giving things away.
3. Get educated as to what sells and for how much; it will save regrets later.
4. Avoid buying or acquiring new stuff. Avoid all sales.
5. Be aware of the sabotages in downsizing: good deals, memories attached, things inherited.
6. Just purge when you finish with something. You don't need to save it.
7. Plan for the future. Be aware of how much space you will have.
8. Get rid of all unimportant paperwork. Shred, recycle, or toss.

Downsizing for me has not been about property. It was about eliminating part of my life as I kept paring down. How could my lifetime be reduced to boxes, storage, and moving vans? Yet I wanted a very simple lifestyle. It meant saying good-bye to things I acquired at different times in my life. My life has been like many other people's journeys—seldom do children or grandchildren want to share all your memories and the things they are attached to, which are uniquely yours. They are doing their own collecting and will understand someday as they, too, downsize and eliminate parts of their lives.

Downsizing Principles

- Cut out the unnecessary.
- Keep the necessary, beautiful, and loved (never let it go; someone else can throw it all away when you're gone). Just be sure you don't leave a huge task—only the best of the best. Anything that can be purchased again is just clutter. The rest are treasures.
- Choose comfortable furniture and kitchen items you actually use.
- Reduce clothing by half or less—easy for most people.
- Decide to take care of "you" and those you love, not stuff or things that might be needed someday. You have enough to do.

Following is a sampling of items that helped me decide to downsize to the simple life:

- Crystal collection and one set of family dishes that tell a three-generation story.
- Memory-filled pillows and afghans, all made by my mother.

- 110 scrapbooks of photos, letters and stories that go back seven generations on my mother's side and two on my father's side, plus movies and slides.
- A Santa Claus made by my son, special gifts made or purchased by my daughters, and any gift from a grandchild.
- All handmade objects (wall hangings) made by a daughter and son-in-law.
- All gifts by another daughter who knows just what I love.
- My collection of angels.
- All beautiful jewelry given to me by my soul mate.

I found it helpful to let go of things when I took photos of especially loved items and put them in a scrapbook. They included my beautiful stained-glass windows commissioned as artwork for our home. There was no way to move them, so we left them behind for the new owners to enjoy. My white furniture, my thirty-five rose bushes, the mountains and golf course in the backyard. I also have special photos of my last four homes, my personal four-season collection. Then I could comfortably say good-bye.

What came with me was limited pieces of white wicker furniture, my 110 family and coupleship scrapbooks, my treasured signed books, most gifts—such as afghans, quilts, crystal, paintings, and wall hangings—the apple dishes, and my favorite clothing.

I am here until the next move.

AGING IN PLACE

If you, as a caregiver or caree, can live a simple life in a simple way, you just might be able to live in beauty, function, and simplicity for many years of your life, which might go on for a long time. Plan for it. Prepare for it and do it. Add travel, hobbies, time off work, and a slow retirement plan. Many people choose to stay where they are as they grow older, whether or not they need caregiving.

Staying in place, which is aging in your home, requires considerable organizational skills. The ideal is for the person staying in place to do it themselves. Should something happen—an accident, illness, or dementia—it becomes necessary for an informed case manager/caregiver who is trained to allow one to continue to age in place by developing a group of caregivers (minor and major). Staying in one's home is the preferred way to live for most people, but when receiving care becomes a necessity, a shortage of money and housing issues prevents this from being practical. Granted, many people feel restricted in a formal setting or a graduated care facility, but sometimes ability and health dictate the choice into this setting.

If you have chosen to age in place, begin early preparation, with the help of your family and service providers, to give yourself a head start in making sure your home and lifestyle are organized in case of illness or accident. Some of the early changes to make can include the following:

- a main floor bedroom
- handicap bars in all the bathrooms
- a list of providers and first call for help
- transportation options set up

INDEPENDENT LIVING

Aging in place is an option that many people choose and handle successfully. The first move after that will probably be to some form of independent living. It often involves moving from a home to a condo, where outside maintenance is handled by the HOA. This is a big move for people, as it's the first move from total independence to a journey of graduated types of independence. Most people postpone this move as long as possible; sometimes it's made in a crisis mode.

The best way to move to this kind of care is by choice, so it's often made before the crisis of need happens. Research the options to find the living situation that best fits your needs. Once you've made the decision, the fun and downsizing challenge begins. What to keep and what to say good-bye to?

INDEPENDENT GRADUATED CARE IN A FACILITY

The next step is often independent graduated facility care. There are two motivators for choosing graduated living as well. One is personal preference, and the other is ability. Residents can start out in an independent setting, then move into assisted living, next to nursing care, and finally to hospice.

Caregivers can do a great service to their carees by helping them learn all the choices and mechanics of making a downsizing decision. Some people love the amenities in the facilities, knowing where someone will live out their days, the letting go of day-to-day cares. Some facilities arrange medical appointments, outings, social events, and countless activities. Again, it is a specialized area of caregiving that helps individuals and families consider and choose from the available options.

END OF LIFE CARE

As most people learn during a hospital event, whether from accident or illness, it is short-lived and needs to be closely managed.

Carees will need help with the management of chronic illness. Palliative service provides comprehensive and compassionate care. It can take place at home or in a facility, such as a nursing home, hospital, or approved hospice facilities. It's all about adding quality of life to individuals and families. A caregiving hospice team can include a range of professionals, volunteers, clergy, nurses, and social workers. Hospice care is covered, at this time, by Medicare and other plans.

It is important to stay up-to-date with coverage, plans, and availability for palliative and hospice candidates. Usually family members become somewhat involved in this decision and work with a caregiver. If no family members are involved, a caregiver working with a professional team have as their primary goal keeping patients comfortable and pain free.

Downsizing is a journey. I currently live in my aging in place, a small condo. My next part of the journey will be graduated care. First, an independent room or set of rooms in an independent living facility and then, when necessary, assisted living, possible memory care, palliative, or hospice care. Circumstances, health, and personal decision will be a part of each move.

It's a complicated journey, and we all will be in some sort of decision-making places for the rest of our lives. May we walk carefully and joyfully into each stage. May our families and dear friends take the walk with us.

MAKE THE BEST OF THE REST AS YOU AGE

"At some point, you gotta let go, and sit still, and
allow contentment to come to you."
—*Elizabeth Gilbert*

We are all headed in the same direction in this life. We are born, we experience joy and disappointments, high times and low times as we journey. We all end up at the same destination. We eventually return to the earth, one way or another. It's only our journeys that are a bit different. To reap all the rewards, do your best to take connection and comforts from the journey.

It's like being on a train. The engine—whatever you believe is the driving force in life—drives us all. Each of us is in a different car, and each car is very different. Some are fancy, some are sparse, some are crowded, and all hold a variety of occupants. Each person will arrive at the same destination. Some will arrive first, and others toward the back of the train will arrive later. Each ride and each rider is unique and different.

We start changing the minute we are born. We face different circumstances and experience a variety of unique events, each one molding and altering our thoughts and ideas. Along our unique journey of life, we continue to age. Each day moves us closer to our final day, when we die.

We live in ever-changing systems and always need to find our way, reframing as we go. The same is true with the life process until it ends.

The important way we can get the best for ourselves and our carees is to communicate about all that is happening in regard to the caree's needs. Being a caregiver presents special challenges in communicating about difficult issues. It helps no one to run away from the challenge. As each stage of the caree's life progresses, the caregiver may feel like he or she is going in circles, wondering what need to fulfill next. The caree may develop fear and become defensive, afraid of losing the essence of who he or she is.

Keep talking and sharing about the delicate things. Keeping important things unspoken helps no one. Following is a list of to-dos for navigating the important times in the later leg of life's journey:

1. Talk openly about hard things.
2. Be clear and straightforward, and bring up one thing at a time.
3. Choose times to talk when both caregiver and caree have the time to listen.
4. Let each other know some discussions or decisions cannot be postponed.
5. Think about quality of life at all times.

GREAT ACTS ARE MADE UP OF SMALL DEEDS

In July 2012, I went to visit my younger sister in Minnesota and was shocked to find that she was seriously ill. She had been sharing with me by phone that she had first one thing that was not right, and then she would call with another thing that didn't seem right.

So I went to visit and spent a week with her. She rallied that week, and we did fun activities. She said that she must have gotten over what was bothering her. We ate barbecue ribs, played board games and cards, and had long talks. She wanted me to go to lunch and see where she worked and meet her co-workers.

After a week, she said she was fine, so I returned home to Nevada. As the summer passed, she called many times, sometimes five times a week, with different things that didn't feel good. My soul mate was ill at home, and many times I felt pulled between my husband's needs and my sister's calls. Both seemed to have more going on than seemed "normal." By fall, my sister sounded more desperate. The symptoms had returned, and my concern was growing. I flew back to Minnesota again and was shocked to find that my sister had been hospitalized. She looked and acted very different to me—withdrawn and secretive. I learned later that she had been diagnosed with cancer and had known for some time. She had made the doctors promise not to tell me.

She was released from the hospital. In shock over her condition, I made preparations to drive her directly to the emergency room at the Mayo Clinic, about five hours away. I made a bed for her in the back of our car, with her favorite pillows and blanket. In torrential rain, we headed down the road. She insisted at stopping at her home to set the recorder for the fall TV series she liked.

The next days are a painful blur. The doctors insisted on many tests and offered several options. She refused all treatment and chose home hospice. The family gathered, along with four of her chosen friends. She refused to see out-of-town visitors.

My daughter held my sister together, and my son held me together. While at the clinic, before she entered hospice, I would get her out of bed and we'd walk together around the nurses' station. She was so weak, I held her up. My sister said that she was "sorry for things she had done to me that weren't fair." She told stories and laughed; it was precious time. I was speechless except to tell her I loved her as we remembered some of our times together.

My sister was released from the clinic and my son and I walked along her gurney, each holding one hand, and watched her being loaded into a medevac to go home. I never saw her again. My daughter and my brother helped with home hospice and my brother was with her when she died on October 13, 2012. It took me five years and professional therapy to process that particular caregiving experience.

Another major caregiving role for me was with my mother, who died of heart disease at a very early age. Caregiving in this case was not day-to-day but from a distance. She was a widow, and we lived in different states. I helped by paying some of her utilities at her condo and going for visits. She loved my children and wanted to see them. She would also come stay with me. I had all of the feelings of guilt: wishing we lived closer, losing her relatively early when she was in her sixties, and having had a complicated relationship.

Following a family intervention, my mother went through treatment that gave her seven years of a very happy life before she died. Family love, complication, and caregiving are a frequent combination.

No one really knows how to be the best caregiver, personally or professionally. We all learn with each experience. It's best to hold hands while we do it. While I use that term, I vividly remember what my mother's hands and my sister's hands looked like. As caregivers give help to carees, it's good to remember these events, because some day they, too, will become the caree.

"My experience is to show appreciation, forgive many events,
and make the best of the rest at every age."
—*Sharon Cruse*

Memories that matter are formed in the days and nights of caregiving and receiving. Sometimes making those memories are all that will remain and time will stop. It isn't usually the camel ride at the pyramids, the island vacation, or an exotic trip of any kind that fills our hearts and souls. It more often is the smells of cooking, laughter in the air, and sharing and crying together that stays with us in the privacy of our souls. Make memories during this special time together. The essence of life is right here. Be in the moment, live in peace, enjoy time with nurturing people, and remember that caregiving involve some of the best years of your life.

DEATH ENDS A LIFE
BUT NOT A RELATIONSHIP

Death leaves a pain no one can heal;
love leaves a memory no one can steal.

—Anonymous

Death is final. Manners of deaths are as varied as lives. Some accidents or attacks result in immediate death. A sudden, unexpected, and untimely death is hard on caregivers and loved ones. My father's sudden death on Christmas Eve was a traumatic event. My uncle's death on Christmas shocked his family. My cousins' deaths in a collision were shocking for all involved. Sometimes it takes years to grieve a sudden death.

Some deaths are relatively fast. My sister's death occurred within a matter of a few weeks. It left us all reeling in a similar way to sudden death. Because of unfinished business and questions, it took some of us years to grieve. Some deaths are lingering and we aren't sure when the actual event will happen. Preparation can be helpful in grieving, or it can lead to complications that intensify grieving. There are really no predictable patterns.

Caregivers and family members have the opportunity to support and aid the person in the transition. Death pulls us in, wrenches attention from us, and then we have to let go. Watching someone in our care or love die is rarely easy. It's a part of reality that the person who dies has either made all their arrangements prior to death or left the remaining family to attend to immediate issues.

Most people would rather not talk about death, but there is no way around it. Everyone, at some time, will face death—their own or someone near to them. It's doubly hard if you love this person and you must make arrangements while grief stricken. It's always too early until it's too late.

It's always too early until it's too late.

The wise, but often considered just lucky, people who have thought about their own deaths, put their wishes and affairs in writing, and gave copies to family members, an attorney, and a caregiver is the preferred way to plan for death. However, only a few have undertaken this journey. Some caregivers are especially trained to help in this process. Attending an "end of life" series of workshops this year was one of the most satisfying learning experiences I have had. As a caregiver, please encourage yourself and your family members to each prepare for their deaths as soon as they are adults. Hopefully, children will always have parents or guardians who will care for them. All adults are wise to have their desires in writing, and, as a caregiver, you can help them prepare.

It would be best, in our culture, if planning for our deaths were part of the "coming of age" process.

Accidents can happen at any age, and illnesses can sneak up on both the young and the old. All preparedness is dual purposed: for the person and for those who are part of that person's life. When a young person dies, the family is distraught. Their suffering is a bit lessened when they know that their young person had a say in his or her death.

Family A lost their fourteen-year-old son to a drowning accident. The family suffered loss the rest of their lives because they felt he never had any choices. They felt empty as they pushed on in life, trying to recover. Everything feels sad in this family, even today as I write about it years later. The parents and their surviving children never talk about death. Therefore, none have made death preparations.

Family B held a family meeting with all their children over the age of twelve and asked them what they experienced about death so far in their young lives. The seventeen-year-old knew a friend who was killed in a car accident, and the thirteen-year-old had lost a beloved dog. The twelve-year-old had lost the family kitten. They talked a bit about loss, and each member listed one thing they would want to have happen at their deaths. One chose to have money given to the Humane Society, one wanted to give a puppy to his best friend Mike, and one said he would let them know the decision by Christmas. It was a meaningful exchange in the family.

When one of the grandparents died, the family decided to apply what the children would choose if they died. Each child donated some money to the Humane Society and wrote a poem for their grandpa. The whole family could talk about death and their feelings, while also taking positive actions about it. The power of choice helped their grieving process.

TOOLS FOR THE CAREGIVER WHEN DEATH OCCURS

Some caregiver tools are applicable when helping a caree or family member prepare for the talk about death. Ellen Goodman, the columnist, has written a great booklet about talking about death called "Have You Had the Conversation Yet?" It is also available on the Internet and billed as The Conversation Project. Many similar projects, books, and kits are available.

It may be that an accident, illness, lack of capacity, or circumstances may interrupt our plans in this regard, so making plans "now" is a good idea. I have a sign on my office door that says, "You might as well try to enjoy now, because it's always now." That is so true and "someday" never really comes. Someday is really now.

The Do-It-Now List

Create an end-of-life folder file or box, and tell three people about it. The file or box should contain the following information:

- where you would like your body sent upon death
- how to call the coroner (include phone number)
- whether you want cremation, viewing, by whom, and a service or memorial—Do you want your ashes buried with headstone or scattered? If scattered, where do you want them? If buried, where to you want them buried and with what epitaph?

- details for the previous information
- names and phone numbers of those to be notified
- legal copies of advance directives
- legal copies of financial power of attorney
- legal copies of medical power of attorney
- name and phone number of your attorney
- name and phone number of your accountant
- a written will, no matter what your age
- if important, a trust

ESTABLISH YOUR PERSONAL LEGACY

Some people like to prepare a number of other written documents. You could also leave a copy of each in your end-of-life file or box. Some ideas include the following:

- values you want to leave behind
- your spiritual views
- political views

DURING THE DYING PROCESS

When you say good-bye the final time, it's important to speak only the words, and use inflections, that you want the dying person to know. No one really knows when sound and comprehension end. The dying person needs only to know comfort.

- Keep the dying person warm and comfortable.

- Touch the person as often as you can. Many say that the sensation of touch is the last thing that stops when someone dies.
- Some dying people are comforted by music. Some crave silence or quiet works. Some prefer prayers. What is important is that you "be there."

What to do at the time of death:

- You have about twelve hours in most states to call the coroner. Check what the rule is in your state. Death is not an emergency.
- Contact people important to the person who died.
- Call the person/agency who will pick up the body.
- Then rest and comfort or be comforted.

First things first once you have rested:

- Do your best to follow through on the person's wishes and desires.
- Be very careful with pre-paying. There are documented cases of not being able to get exactly what you paid for, the funeral home has closed down, or you are forced to pay a premium.
- Shop around and ask people you know for personal referrals and past experiences.
- Try not to do anything alone. You are greatly vulnerable at this time, and a team effort is best used in this situation. Give everyone a job. It helps them in their grieving process to have something to do.

CELEBRATE THE LIFE OF THE PERSON WHO HAS DIED

Follow the person's wishes. This was one of the most difficult parts of my sister's death. She asked that no one gather, that we not have a service or memorial, and that we accept this is what she wanted. It was a very difficult choice for the family. I had to find other ways to celebrate her life while honoring her wishes.

For those who want a funeral, make any arrangements they requested. If they didn't leave any instructions, simply use good judgment. Observe any tradition that is important to the deceased and family, such as sitting Shiva or having a wake.

For those who chose cremation, the opportunity is to have a celebration/memorial when it's convenient for you and the family. Not everyone will be able to be there; do the best you can. Creativity abounds when it comes to death memorials. To honor someone's memory is to bring a little piece of them to the memorial.

Ways I Have Experienced to Celebrate a Life

- Play great music they loved.
- Let their dog or pet attend.
- Have friends and family speak and read.
- Let guests share memories.
- Make a toast with the person's favorite wine.
- Celebrate Mass (for Catholics).
- Hold a candlelight ceremony.
- Create a photo display.
- Make decorations.

- Serve party food.
- Drive around the neighborhood in a limo or car, saying good-bye publicly for the person.
- Wear funny glasses and dance to "When the Saints Go Marching In."
- Show a video or DVD of the person and some of the life they lived.
- Let creativity reign.

RITUALS AND FINAL CHAPTERS

- Choose a family historian and decide to save whatever brings comfort.
- Select something that can be shared with those who share the loss, and give out at the funeral, memorial, or gathering any of the following:
  - memory cards
  - a photo, family album, or history
  - a program to be shared with all those who care
- Set up a virtual connection for those who want to attend but are unable to.

Fun Summaries of Life in Six Words or Less

- Almost gave up; glad I didn't.
- Living my bucket list—gratitude.
- Start over again, again, and again.
- Keep going—life unfolds.
- Kindness goes a long way.
- Experience every day as special.

- Sometimes difficult—but worth it.
- Been there, done that—often enough.
- I took the road less traveled.
- The best is yet to come: forever.
- Birth, life, learning, and peace.
- Making a difference is fulfillment.
- Lesson after lesson after lesson—smile.
- Live Daily—Learn—Love Always.

NO REGRETS: THE BEST LIFE

*The past is finished. There is nothing
to be gained by going over it. Whatever it gave
us in the experiences it brought us was
something we had to know.*

—Rebecca Beard

Over the last few weeks and months, this book has been a driving force for me. It's become my friend. Writing fills my heart and my soul and comforts my very being. From my computer, high on the second floor of my home, beauty and friendship fill my soul. Looking out the window, I see trees, sky, and clouds. Most days I can see the horizon miles away. Looking below, I view people, dogs, and green grass—and sometimes everything is covered in snow. I feel a deep sense of connection in all parts of life. I hope I get a great many years more of enjoying the view.

With the outside scene, the inside quiet, my favorite music flowing from my Bose speakers, my feelings are intense, alive. Looking around the meditation area in the corner, I note that everything in the room except two rocking chairs, a Keurig coffee/tea maker, and my radio are gifts. Life doesn't get much better than this. I hope it's in my destiny to have a great many days like this. My giant calendar is filled with many things to look forward to, including a great deal of caregiving.

My plans are to be the best caregiver I can be, take the best care of myself, deepen a few friendships, greet every person I encounter (I especially love to connect with waiters), be kind to my own caregivers, write more, and connect with those I love and am loved by. This will involve a bit of audacity and plain speaking, trying to finish unfinished business wherever I can, and hugging those who want to be hugged.

At this age and stage, I have razor-sharp focus. No real time for anything nonessential and not part of my value system.

At this age and stage, I have razor-sharp focus. No real time for anything nonessential and not part of my value system.

There is not enough time—there never is. Knowing I will never be bored, my focus will be on myself, my family, God's will, and my dear friends. I have less time for opinionated personalities, news broadcasts, and unproductive pursuits on the computer. It's not indifference, it's more like detachment from earthly things and clinging to the important things.

Realizing that I define what's important to me, I point to injustice to people of any race, color, or creed. I care for children and animals; global warming. Politics are still a passion for me—not talking about them but choosing to live them. Taking care of the people entrusted to me and saving the earth matters.

I have experienced cancer, heart disease, and a diabetes scare. I am aware of the impact of lung and heart illnesses, accidents, and Parkinson's disease on my nearest and dearest. I know my time is finite. So is yours, my beloved caregiver and caree. Use it wisely and live with a "no regrets lifestyle." My good fortune and longing has taken me to all the places on my bucket list that were very important to me. I haven't been everywhere; I don't need to do it all. Today, my experiences have filled my heart and soul with laughter; funny family stories; showing up whenever and however I could; celebrating holidays, birthdays, and traditions; and remembering and contacting people. My illnesses happened more than twenty-five years ago, and they were gifts that taught me what is truly important to me.

> "Tell me, what is it you plan to do with your
> one wild and precious life?"
> —Mary Oliver

As each day, week, and month goes by, it's clear that we all travel a private journey. Watching people run around, travel constantly, suffer physical symptoms way too often, and work way too hard teaches me the joy of satisfaction, relationship, purpose, and inner peace. At my age, I have watched many of my family and friends die. In recent times, I have watched far too many young people die, not getting the chance to enjoy the journey of aging. Each death of someone I know is a bit of an abruption to what I know. Caregiving sees death often. No one can be replaced. Death leaves holes that cannot be filled.

Caregivers get the opportunity to feel gratitude for a life fully lived. We love, are loved, and have been loved. We have given much and received much. There is a great deal of gratitude for having the honor of caregiving.

Sometimes at a stoplight or in a grocery store, I look around to the people near me and wonder which ones have been or are the caregivers in the world. I can almost guess, as it's easy to feel the depth and the humanness that connects parents, pet lovers, and caregivers. It's a special kind of passion and commitment one can feel with another. For this, I am grateful.

> "You should never view your challenges as a disadvantage.
> It's important to understand your experience facing and overcoming adversity is actually one of your biggest advantages."
> —*Michelle Obama*

Afterthoughts

*W*ho would ever have thought that . . .

My greatest and most difficult book I have ever written is this one?

I could ever get so angry and feel so much love at the same time?

My meat loaf and macaroni-and-cheese kind of guy would end up liking fruit, cereal, and granola?

The very private me would be telling personal family stories?

I could be so mellow, accepting, and feel I am living "my bucket list" and am filled with gratitude?

I am becoming one of the angels I have always believed came to me?

I could ever feel so alone and connected at the same time?

I would adopt three caregivers into my inner circle when I have protected my privacy all my life?

I could live each day comfortably with what has been, is now, and will yet come?

Some days the disappointments, hurts, fears, sorrows are so present that I can't breathe, and yet on those days, I know there will be a tomorrow.

New neighbors of just five years provide me with a lifetime of love?

This family therapist that I am, still waits eagerly for my bimonthly meeting with my therapist, who provides me with tools and great joy?

A beautiful, much younger, and much more productive woman would arrive at my door, and I am eager to invite her to come in (actually three times a week)?

Caregiving, with all the stress and strain (filled with emotional baggage), provides me a more wonderful life than I could have ever known any other way?

In losing parts of myself, I have found other parts of myself, and the "whole package deal" is a treasure. Don't be afraid of the "package deal."

Resources

B elow are books, organizations, and websites that I have found helpful.

TOOLS FOR WORKING WITH SENIORS

Carnarius, Megan, *A Deeper Perspective on Alzheimer's and Other Dementia,* Rochester, VT: Findhorn Press, 2015

Gayatri, Devi, MD, *The Spectrum of Hope,* New York: Workman Press, 2017

Merriman, Melanie P., *Holding the Net,* Brattleboro, VT: Green Writers Press, 2017

Pohl, Mel, and Ketcham, Katherine, *The Pain Antidote,* Boston: DaCapo Lifelong Press, 2015

Sheehy, Gail, *Passages in Caregiving,* New York: HarperCollins, 2010

Smits, Angel, *When Reasoning No Longer Works,* Colorado Springs: Parker Hayden Media, 2017

Waichler, Iris, *Role Reversal: How to Take Care of Yourself and Your Aging Parents,* Berkeley, CA: She Writes Press, 2016

TOOLS FOR WORKING WITH A SPOUSE

Abbit, Linda, *The Conscious Caregiver:* New York: Simon & Schuster, 2017

Denholm, Diana B., *The Caregiving Wife's Handbook,* Alameda, CA: Hunter House, 2012

Peel, Rosalys, *Mike and Me,* Wallace, ID: Zadra Publishing, 2018

Schreiber, Martin, and Breitenbucher, Cathy, *My Two Elaines,* Bothell, WA: Book Publishers Network, 2018

Williams, Patricia, *While They Are Still Here,* Berkeley, CA: She Writes Press, 2018

TOOLS TO HELP THE CAREGIVER PERSONALLY

Gayatri, Devi, MD, *The Spectrum of Hope,* New York: Workman Press, 2017

Jacobs, Barry J., and Mayer, Julie L., *Meditations for Caregivers,* Boston: DaCapo Press, 2016

Mace, Nancy L., and Robins, Peter V., *The 36 Hour Day,* Baltimore, MD: Johns Hopkins University Press, 1981

Weckworth, Nancy, *Don't Stop the Music: Find Joy in Caregiving,* Bloomington, IN: Balboa Press, 2015

TOOLS FOR PREPARING FOR END-OF-LIFE ISSUES

Munn, Rebecca Whitehead, *The Gift of Goodbye,* Berkeley, CA: She Writes Press, 2018

Fortuna, Michael, *Caregiver Defined,* Saverio Press, 2017

ORGANIZATIONS AND WEBSITES

Websites Related to Aging Issues

Rosalynn Carter Institute for Caregiving: *www.rosalynncarter.org*

National Organization for Empowering Caregivers: *www.care-givers.com*

Eldercare Locater: *www.eldercare.acl.gov*

National Associations for Home Care and Hospice: *www.nahc.org*

Family Caregiver Alliance: *www.caregiver.org*

Embracing Carers: *www.embracingcarers.com/en_US/home.html*

Caregiving.Com: *www.caregiving.com*

Disease-Related Websites

National Parkinson Foundation: *www.parkinson.org*

The Mended Hearts, Inc.: *www.mendedhearts.org*

Myasthenia Gravis Foundation: *www.myasthenia.org*

Cancer Care: *www.cancercare.org*

Arthritis Foundation: *www.arthritis.org*

Many illnesses have websites by using their name and *www.theirname.org*

National Resources

Aging with Dignity: *www.agingwithdignity.org*

American Association of Retired Persons: *www.aarp.org*

Caring Connections: *www.caringinfo.org*

Have You Had the Conversation Yet?: *www.theconversationproject.org*

Age Well Academy: *www.iona.org/services/take-charge-age-well-academy/*

The Gray Panthers: *www.graypanthersnyc.org*

SAGE (LGBT Seniors): *www.sageusa.org*

Conscious Eldering: *www.centerforconsciouseldering.com*

Age Well Global: *www.agewellglobal.com*

Meals on Wheels: *www.mealsonwheelsamerica.org*

RetireWow: *www.retirewow.com*

Love to Know: *seniors.lovetoknow.com*

Technology and Aging

Tech for Caregivers: *www.techthatcares.com*

Aging 2.0: *www.aging2.com*

Seniors Guide to Computers: *www.seniorsguidetocomputers.com*

Age in Place Technology: *www.ageinplacetech.com*

Senior Net: *www.seniornet.org*

Senior Planet: *seniorplanet.org*

Oasis Lifelong Adventure: *https://www.oasisnet.org*

TechBoomers: *https://techboomers.com*

ALL BOOKS, ALPHABETICAL BY AUTHOR

Abbit, Linda, *The Conscious Caregiver,* New York: Simon & Schuster, 2017

Carnarius, Megan, *A Deeper Perspective on Alzheimer's and Other Dementia,* Rochester, VT: Findhorn Press, 2015

Denholm, Diana B., *The Caregiving Wife's Handbook,* Alameda, CA: Hunter House, 2012

Fortuna, Michael, *Caregiver Defined,* Saverio Press, 2017

Gayatri, Devi, MD, *The Spectrum of Hope,* New York: Workman Press, 2017

Jacobs, Barry J., and Mayer, Julie L., *Meditations for Caregivers,* Boston: DaCapo Press, 2016

Mace, Nancy L., and Robins, Peter V., *The 36 Hour Day*, Baltimore, MD: Johns Hopkins University Press, 1981

Merriman, Melanie P., *Holding the Net*, Brattleboro, VT: Green Writers Press, 2017

Munn, Rebecca Whitehead, *The Gift of Goodbye*, Berkeley, CA: She Writes Press, 2018

Peel, Rosalys, *Mike and Me*, Wallace, ID: Zadra Publishing, 2018

Pohl, Mel, and Ketcham, Katherine, *The Pain Antidote*, Boston: DaCapo Lifelong Press, 2015

Schreiber, Martin, and Breitenbucher, Cathy, *My Two Elaines*, Bothell, WA: Book Publishers Network, 2018

Sheehy, Gail, *Passages in Caregiving*, New York: HarperCollins, 2010

Smits, Angel, *When Reasoning No Longer Works*, Colorado Springs: Parker Hayden Media, 2017

Waichler, Iris, *Role Reversal: How to Take Care of Yourself and Your Aging Parents*, Berkeley, CA: She Writes Press, 2016

Weckworth, Nancy, *Don't Stop the Music: Find Joy in Caregivin*, Bloomington, IN: Balboa Press, 2015

Williams, Patricia, *While They Are Still Here*, Berkeley, CA: She Writes Press, 2018

For more information on this book,
the topic of caregiving, and the authors, visit:
www.CaregivingHopeAndHealth.com

Index

An *f* following a page number indicates a figure.

Index

234   Index

C

Caree, 51–52. *See also* Basic caregiver
    and caree needs; Boundaries,
    setting practical; Ongoing
    caregiver and caree needs;
    Thriving caregiver and caree
    needs
  changes for, 53
  communication between caregiver
    and, 54–55
  identifying, 54
  patterns of behavior, 56
  private space for, 111
  separating person from illness,
    91–92, 97–98
  with special needs, 69
Caregivers. *See also* Basic caregiver and
    caree needs; Ongoing caregiver
    and caree needs; Thriving
    caregiver and caree needs
  asking for help, 87–88
  characteristics of, 26–27
  choosing to love, 97–98
  communication between caree and,
    54–55
  examples of challenges in, 13–21
  family members not helping, xvii–
    xviii
  family support, 19
  friends as, 32–33, 48
  grandparents as, 49–50
  hats of, 17*f*
  identifying the, 25–27
  isolation of, 20
  mentors and heroes as, 72–78
  nonfood rewards, 106
  oneself as, 14
  paid, 27, 29–30
  private-pay, 33–35
  professionals, 10–11, 188–191
  rewards of, 27
  roles in family, 40–42
  self-care, tools for, 178–180
  sleeping problems, 14

spouse feels abandoned, 16
tips for eating, 106–107
types of, 10
weight gain in, 14, 15, 16
when death occurs, tools for
    caregiver, 214–215
what they miss, xvii–xix
Caregiving. *See also* Caregiving burnout
  as business, 12
  during dying process, 215–216
  financial, 71–72
  general principles for, 101
  hope, 90
  with least engagement, 20–21
  long distance, 70
  need for arising, 12–13
  symptoms of burnout, 79–81
  system dynamics, 44
  technology and, 137–144
  volunteers in, 45–47, 50
Caregiving burnout
  anger, 81–83
  fear, 83–84
  grief, 84
  guilt, 81
  magical thinking, 86–87
  signs and symptoms of serious,
    84–87
  shame, 83
Communication
  between caree and caregiver, 54–55
  between caregiving agencies and
    media, 7–8
  family, xvii, 149
  in troubled world, 191–192
Conflict, tools for handling
  judging oneself on rank, 132
  knowing how much to share, 132–
    133
  old feelings and hurts, 131
  red-flag subjects, 131
  timing, 130
Crisis
  communication and structure in, 7–8